Our
Changing
LITURGY

Our Changing LITURGY

by C. J. McNaspy, S.J.

with a Foreword by
Godfrey Diekmann, O.S.B.

CATHOLIC
PERSPECTIVES

General Editor: John J. Delaney

HAWTHORN BOOKS *Publishers* **NEW YORK**

First Edition: January, 1966

IMPRIMI POTEST

John J. McGinty, S.J.
Praepositus Prov. Neo-Eborac.

NIHIL OBSTAT

Myles M. Bourke, S.S.L., S.T.D.
Censor Librorum

IMPRIMATUR

Terence J. Cooke, V.G.

New York, New York
October 26, 1965

The nihil obstat and the imprimatur are official declarations that a book or pamphlet is free of doctrinal or moral error. No implication is contained therein that those who have granted the nihil obstat and imprimatur agree with the contents, opinions or statements expressed.

6930

Contents

TO

FATHERS GERALD AND AUGUSTINE ELLARD

AND

WILLIAM J. LEONARD

Foreword

$\mathcal{M}$ore and more it is becoming clear what a "happy accident" it was that Vatican Council II chose the schema on the liturgy for its first major topic of discussion, and that the Constitution on the Sacred Liturgy was consequently the first of the great documents to be solemnly promulgated. A chief result of this temporal priority was the influence the liturgy document exerted on the subsequent discussion on the Church, and on the final formulation of the splendid Constitution on the Church which issued from the third session of the Council in November, 1964. It is a matter of record that the first draft of the text on the Church was rejected by the Council Fathers not least of all because its ecclesiology did not measure up to that already approved in the liturgy document.

Public interest, it is true, centered largely on the question of the collegiality of bishops, and the exercise of their authority in relation to the primacy of Peter. No one would question the importance of this problem. And yet it may be doubted whether it will equal in long-range significance the Council's emphasis on the Church as "the people of

God," and on the active role and responsibility of every one of its members, whether laity or hierarchy. The Constitution on the Liturgy and the Constitution on the Church establish a historic declaration of the rights of full citizenship on the part of every baptized member of the Church, in worship first, and then in the full range of the Church's activity.

Declaration, however, is one thing; putting it into practice is quite another. The layman is now solemnly called upon to collaborate according to his talents, and according to the spiritual gifts and powers committed to him by God; and the hierarchy, bishops and priests, are reminded not merely of their authority, but of the Christian meaning of authority as above all a ministering to God's holy people, in the common effort of upbuilding the Church. The new Pentecost hoped for by Pope John will become a reality to the extent that the entire people of God, priests and laymen, will become fully engaged in Christ's task according to their respective roles and gifts.

But how spell out, in the concrete, this actively contributive role of the layman in the parish, in the diocese, in the Church, in the world? How is he to be consulted, how is his initiative to be guaranteed and put to best use? What changes in the normal life and administration of the parish, diocese, and universal Church are necessary or most apt to effectuate a Body of Christ duly active in all its parts? This is the challenge confronting the Church honestly seeking self-reform and rejuvenation. These are the big questions posed by Vatican Council II and the future years of implementation.

Again we can be grateful that the Constitution on the Liturgy was promulgated first, for it does give a definite answer to these questions in their most important dimension: that of the Church's task of worship. And the answer is concrete enough to allow its being put into practice immediately. The ancient principle of "distribution of roles" is restored, and its application indicated in detail. Moreover, if the laity learn to exercise their worship rights *and* by this experience achieve the essential Christian sense of community and of consequent social responsibilities, this cannot but better dispose them for their further involvement in the Church's activities.

The year that has elapsed since the promulgation of the Constitution on the Liturgy has, however, pointed up another problem: though an answer has been given, not all have been ready to accept it. Habit, especially in religious practices, exercises a momentum of exceptional force. And even fifty years of the liturgical movement were insufficient to reach all, much less to convince them of the need of improvement through change. But we cannot afford to wait another fifty years. The Church has spoken through the Council, and is asking for liturgical renewal now, as the foundation of her own hoped-for spiritual revitalization.

This is the situation that Father McNaspy has set out to meet in writing his book. And meet it he does, with eminent success. I would therefore ask the reader to pay no attention to Father McNaspy's humble protestations in the Introduction to this volume. It may be true that there is an encouragingly large number of books on the liturgy available today; but his book fills a specific and presently urgent need—"to help the troubled layman find some perspective amid the changes that face him every time he goes to church." And I suspect that many priests as well as laymen will profit from it and be grateful to the author for having written it. Nor will its usefulness be limited to this present time of adjustment. The answers given are based on a sound grasp of principles, stated more convincingly because Father McNaspy draws upon the wide range of his other interests.

For Father McNaspy is a man equally at home in half a dozen or more areas of thought and endeavor. I first met him when he, a Jesuit, was lecturing on Gregorian chant in a Benedictine abbey (which would, however, be a lesser reason for surprise today than it was a mere decade ago!); and every discussion with him since then has been a further discovery of his expert knowledge in a variety of fields.

When he asked me to write the Foreword to this book, I could not say no; for, as his many other friends will be able to testify, he has the annoying habit of always outdoing one in generosity, so that one feels permanently indebted. Now that I have read his volume I am doubly happy that I consented, because it means not only that I can repay a friend, but that I can have a modest part in launching a book that will advance in no small degree the pastoral realization of the liturgical renewal, and therefore of the Church's new Pentecost.

Godfrey Diekmann, O.S.B.

Collegeville, Minnesota

Introduction

One of the better true stories to come out of Vatican Council II was told me by an unimpeachable witness: It was a morning when the liturgy was being celebrated by the Ethiopians in their own rather piquant rite. A venerable Italian bishop, distressed at such unfamiliar ceremonies carried on near the tomb of St. Peter, could finally no longer contain himself. With a grunt he exclaimed to his neighbor: "What a carnival!" His more permissive confrere shrugged and commented: "Yes, Monsignore, but isn't the whole thing a carnival?" By the whole thing he presumably meant St. Peter's, the Council, and the liturgy.

The anecdote focuses on several of the unresolved—perhaps never-to-be-resolved—tensions that are central to any liturgical discussion. What is the proper element of "carnival" in liturgy or any celebration? When does culture become *Kitsch*? At what point does unity freeze into uniformity? To what extent does catholicity imply diversity? How popular should the mode of worship done by God's people actually be? In liturgy—which is the transaction be-

11

tween God and man—how humanly conditioned ought we to be in our posture, gesture, language, song?

This list of problems is in no way exhaustive. Romano Guardini, surely one of the fathers of the liturgical renewal, gave these problems a most acute formulation in his now celebrated open letter to West Germany's Mainz Liturgical Congress. He asked: "Is not the liturgical act, and with it, all that goes under the name of 'liturgy' so bound up with the historical background—antique or medieval or baroque— that it would be more honest to give it up altogether?" He further asked: "Would it not be better to admit that man in this industrial and scientific age, with its new sociological structure, is no longer capable of a liturgical act? And instead of talking of renewal, ought we not to consider how best to celebrate the sacred mysteries so that modern man can grasp their meaning through his own approach to truth?" [1]

No single book, least of all one of scant dimensions, can hope to answer fully such profound difficulties. Yet, no book can touch on the liturgy as it is being revised today without giving them some serious attention.

At the other pole are difficulties or objections offered, in varying degrees of sophistication and articulateness, by those Catholics who are dismayed by change, especially by the changes in the Mass. These objections range all the way from the robust crudeness of an usher in one of our New York churches who, thinking a visiting Anglican priest to be a Catholic, asked him: "How do you like our *Protestant* service, Father?" to the well-chiseled, acidulous comments of Evelyn Waugh or the laments appearing almost every week among "Letters to the Editor" in the London *Tablet*. Two specific instances of these may be cited:

Dear Sir: Those of us who have always been opposed to an English liturgy must find our worst fears exceeded in the clumsy, inconsistent, ungrammatical text. . . . [September 12, 1964]

Dear Sir: Of course it does not matter whether Mass is said in Tamil or Chinese—better if it were! The trouble with English is that we do understand it and therefore its inadequacies are painfully obvious. [September 19, 1964]

Other letters go even further, objecting not only to English in the liturgy but also to any changes whatever.

In a well-developed article, "The English Catholics," Bernard Bergonzi summed up this attitude of dissatisfaction as he observed it in some British circles: "Many are scandalised. Liturgical changes are impending, and this is already arousing resentment and concern. Many Catholics are attached to the Latin Mass simply because they grew up with it. I am a convinced vernacularist myself, but I recognise that the change-over could be rather traumatic for many admirable but uninformed Catholics." [2] Even, I would add, for some of the informed.

In France, perhaps to no one's surprise, reaction was often more vehement and vocal. In a number of parishes, when the priest gave the greeting *Dominus vobiscum* in French (*Le Seigneur soit avec vous*), he heard a single thunderous response in Latin, *Et cum spiritu tuo*, while the people generally whispered the French equivalent.

The problem is by no means a European one. Among letters that I have received expressing opposition to liturgical

13

changes, one from a teacher in the Chicago area states her feelings with clarity and the sincerity of a *cri du coeur:* "As a member of the laity (of which we are hearing so much and which is still consulted not at all on any of the changes so greatly affecting them) may I say I know no one, layman or priest (and I have a wide circle of friends among both), who is in any way overjoyed. The word might be over-whelmed. We are dismayed. The clergy seem to have no realization of the hold the Mass as we knew it has on so many of us. Why weren't we asked? In more than 50 years of attendance at Mass I have felt no loneliness. I was part of the most beautiful drama in the world. The silence of the old way was one of its beauties. Aren't all mysteries silent things?"

Then, on March 20, 1965, a rather "anonymous" group of Catholics published a manifesto which already had had months of private circulation. This group, called the "Cath-olic Traditionalist Movement," expressed great anxiety over "the first phase of a broader scheme intended to 'protestant-ize' the entire Catholic Church." The manifesto found this conspiracy at work in the efforts of "a small but well organ-ized minority of in their ivory towers isolated self-appointed so-called liturgical experts" (*sic*), who "extorted from the Bishops" the changes that were being imposed on Catholics. Response, the manifesto went on, ranged "from passive resig-nation to outright resentment." No statistics or other evi-dence were offered to bolster this opinion, but there could be no question that the "Traditionalists" felt strongly and expressed passionately their view that the changes were un-popular and clearly for the worse.

Two months before the Traditionalist Manifesto appeared, the San Francisco *Chronicle* invited its Catholic readers to participate in a poll of their views on the changes made in the Mass prior to January 20. At least three deficiencies in the poll weakened its scientific reliability: 1. Some of the questions were weighted against the changes; 2. The results published (on February 2) showed only percentages, with no indication of the number of readers who responded or their breakdown into groupings; 3. It is common knowledge that normally only those readers who are unhappy and wish to protest will take the trouble to fill out a reply and mail it. Even with these reservations, however, some interesting and surprising results emerged.

In the first place, 63 per cent of respondents reported that they favored the introduction of English into the Mass. Further, while only 41 per cent reported being opposed to being asked to join in the responses and prayers, 53 per cent objected that participation "intrudes upon their habit of personal, silent prayer and worship." Further, 55 per cent found that "the abandonment of the all-Latin service deprived the Mass of some of its mystical quality and solemnity." On the other hand, 68 per cent granted that though the English Mass took more time than the Latin, they were not opposed to the greater length.

A more careful study is reported in *Our Tongues Were Loosed,* by John J. Jankauskas. After some ten years of experience presenting the liturgy to the faithful of a lower-middle-class Chicago parish, Father Jankauskas conducted a series of carefully structured interviews with 383 people, meeting in forty-five groups. The response indicated an overwhelming acceptance of the type of participatory and other changes now coming into general use, and almost unanimous enthusiasm for them. In the words of one of the parishioners, the parish under study seemed "the most unlikely spot in the entire archdiocese where participation would flourish." Thus, the techniques described should be of use to anyone, layman or priest, concerned about his own parish.[3]

It is clear, then, that reaction to recent liturgical change cannot be fairly described as unanimously enthusiastic. Opponents, as always, have been vocal. Yet after discussion with many priests in all parts of the country, as well as with a wide spectrum of laity, I find that reaction is generally favorable, and more often than not enthusiastic. Even elderly people, who expressed anxiety about the changes, often find them easy to accept once they experience them. This is not to suggest that problems or concern do not arise even among the most favorably disposed. Were this the case, there would be little need for the present book.

Aware of the dismay or bewilderment of some Catholics at this moment, Pope Paul has repeatedly urged them to make the effort needed to understand the Constitution on the Sacred Liturgy. In a general audience on January 13, 1965, he stated: "The religious and spiritual plane opened to us through the new liturgical Constitution is stupendous." And this, he explained, for several reasons: the depth and authenticity of its teaching; its reasonableness; its cultural implications; and its response to the needs of modern man.

The Holy Father went on to make clear that certain liturgical laws of the past are today inadequate. Accordingly, the Church is courageously trying to bring out the true meaning of liturgy, to deepen its social implications, to stress the worship function of the Word of God as presented in Holy Scripture and the homily.

Again, on March 17, the Holy Father granted that some people are confused by the more recent changes—the presence of new prayers, the absence of old ones; Communion received while standing; the new gestures and the lack of certain old gestures. At the same time, he took nothing away from the

Council's Constitution and the later directives of the Post-conciliar Commission. Instead, he urged everyone to make an effort to overcome the spiritual indolence that prevents understanding of and participation in the "most sacred of religious acts." He added that he had received many communications of enthusiasm from young and old, from the pious and the learned, from all those who were now discovering in this new experience what it meant to really share in the Holy Sacrifice. At the same time, he cautioned against merely becoming used to the new liturgy. For the "liturgical renewal, this spiritual rebirth, cannot take place without cooperation, without willing and earnest preparation."

The very reluctance felt by many exemplary Catholics—traditionalists and others—may be said to have a happy side too. It suggests, perhaps to our surprise, that many persons were not superficial in their response to the "old" liturgy, despite its inadequacies. People would hardly, even out of habit and routine, be so attached to old ways if those ways were not at least partly meaningful. In some instances, at least, resistance may be no more than a natural conservative reaction explainable in terms of background, temperament, or psychic structure. It may even suggest a type of Catholicism far removed from the "soft, inert paste" so often caricatured.[4]

Moreover, the Traditionalists might be more at ease with the changes made by the Council and implementation of them, if they reflected on the number of major changes in liturgical practice that have been made in recent years and to which people generally have become accustomed. The older among us can recall when First Communion was delayed almost to the time of adolescence; many of us can recall when the daily missal came into common use, between the World Wars; all of us surely remember the important changes in the law of the Eucharistic fast. And in regard to the hour when Mass may be said, for example, I recall the distinguished medieval Latinist, Father Otto Kuhnmuench, telling me back in 1937 that I would live to see the day of evening Masses. I thought then that he was letting his optimism get the best of him. No one that I know would propose revoking any of these changes. Yet each of them seemed unthinkable only a few years before it became common practice.

Liturgy is no longer thought of as a personal luxury or private preserve, still less as a mere external duty. Each of us, from the simplest to the most sophisticated, has a need for liturgy. In his admirable preface to Dag Hammarskjold's *Markings,* W. H. Auden put this with great refinement: "It is precisely the introverted intellectual character who stands most in need of the ecclesiastical routine, both as a discipline and a refreshment." And while "ecclesiastical routine" can hardly have been intended as a full description of liturgy, and "refreshment" is only a part of liturgy's role, Auden's point is as clear as it is apt.

This book, while touching on several urgent and exalted themes of contemporary Catholicism, was written with the most modest of aims: simply to help the troubled layman find some perspective amid the changes that face him every time he goes to church. It is thus not meant for the theologian or well-read liturgist, but for the ordinary Catholic who may be suffering from liturgical malaise.

I need hardly say that it was not my intention to enter into rivalry with the many excellent works in the Suggested Reading list included at the end of this book—such volumes, to mention just a few, as J. D. Crichton's commentary on the Constitution on the Sacred Liturgy, *The Church's Wor-*

ship, H. A. Reinhold's *The Dynamics of the Liturgy,*
Charles Davis' *Liturgy and Doctrine,* Godfrey Diekmann's
Come, Let Us Worship, Louis Bouyer's *Liturgical Piety,*
James W. King's *The Liturgy and the Laity,* and I. H.
Dalmais' *Introduction to the Liturgy.* Rather, I should hope
that some of these and other introductory works are at
hand, and that anyone who reads these pages will turn to
them for a fuller, more rounded treatment of the Church's
public worship and the theology on which it is grounded.

My purpose is both more limited and, in all likelihood,
more ephemeral than the others'. It is to cast some scattered
bits of light on today's changing liturgy: on the several
areas of change and their relevance to other vital movements
that the Church is experiencing in our time. In no way is
this to suggest that the liturgy is the only fulcrum on which
these movements meet and interrelate. However, I believe
that our social worship cannot be understood when treated
separately, and that it is shortsighted to view the biblical,
catechetical, social and ecumenical trends of today's Church
in isolation from one another or as unrelated to the liturgical
renewal as a whole. It is plain, too, that reforms in church
art and music are affected by liturgy, even to the extent of
being shaped by it. Hence I have included a chapter on
them.

It was more than whim, accident, or pressure that led the
Council to start its vast encounter with present-day problems by re-examining the Church's worship. For, more than
anything else, the Church is the people of God at worship.
It has often been pointed out that the two principal documents of the Council thus far, the Constitution on the Sacred
Liturgy and the Constitution on the Church, are mutually
complementary: the first, in some ways, is a foreshadowing

of the second and contains much of it in embyro. Throughout the book I have tried to show this interrelationship.

The Suggested Reading list at the end of this book is divided by chapters and is confined to recent books that should be useful to the general reader. It represents a compromise that had to be settled for, somewhere between completeness and a bare minimum. The volumes mentioned in Chapter One are not so much on change as such, as on the basic theology underpinning the liturgical changes put forth in the Constitution on the Sacred Liturgy. While not all of these books are equally easy to read, neither are they excessively technical. For the sake of beginners, I have ventured in the portion for Chapter One to list the titles in what seem a helpful order of introduction, from the simpler to the more difficult. Which one you select to read first will remain your own secret.

It will be noticed that I have avoided any pretense at originality, but have continually drawn on the work of several giant theologians who seem to express the richest Catholic thought of our time, notably men like Fathers Karl Rahner, Edward Schillebeeckx and Charles Davis. A number of helpful references to Rahner's writings I owe to Father Donald Gelpi, whose forthcoming work, *An Introduction to the Theology of Karl Rahner,* I was privileged to read in manuscript. Special thanks, too, are in order to several of my colleagues on the staff of *America* magazine, and to other friends who gave advice and encouragement. Among them are Fathers William J. Leonard, Frederick R. McManus, Donald J. Martin, H. James Yamauchi, Servando Mendez and Rock Caporale, and Mr. Robert Rambusch. I am particularly grateful to the distinguished editor-in-chief of *Worship* magazine, Father Godfrey Diekmann, for his gracious foreword; to the National Catholic Welfare Conference for kind permission to reprint the Constitution on the Liturgy; and to Mr. Maurice Lavanoux, editor of *Liturgical Arts* quarterly, for permission to reprint the *Instruction* and *Appendix* on sacred art.

C.J.McN.

ONE

Changes
in the Church

Recently a friend of mine was escorting a group of visitors around the new cathedral in Baltimore. He pointed to the image of the Last Supper and named each of the Apostles represented, Judas among them. A dear lady asked, without the slightest trace of irony, "Is Judas a saint now too?" My friend reassured her. Unshaken in the Faith, she shrugged: "Oh, Father, I didn't know, with all the changes going on these days."

Back in pre-ecumenical days, long before I had any exposure to theology, I remember taking an equally naïve position at the opposite pole. Arguing with a Protestant friend, I triumphantly pointed to the fact that ours was a totally unchanging church. "For example," I insisted, more polemically than historically, "our priests have been saying Mass since the days of St. Augustine in exactly the same way—words, gestures, and all." I can now plead, in slight exculpation, that I was very young and had been brought up to believe that since the Church was apostolic it could not really have changed in any way and still remain the Church of the Apostles. Why I singled out St. Augustine,

I am not sure. Perhaps I thought he was one of the Apostles.

When Catholic scholars some few decades ago began to discuss openly the need for changes in the liturgy, they faced a general attitude of dismay at the thought of surrendering a single jot or tittle. To those innocent of history, every ceremony, every candle, every stitch of vestment was as untouchable as the Trinity. Even today one meets resistance to any abandonment of the stiff, misnamed "Roman" Chasuble as though it were a part of tradition. (It is, in fact, a rather recent innovation, largely baroque in inspiration, with few traditional or artistic claims on our loyalty.) The decanonization of legendary St. Philomena caused distress in not a few quarters but even stancher devotion in others. (I know one rectory where the pastor proudly displays his relic of the beloved saint, together with a relic of one of the Holy Innocents. Be it said, however, that the holy man is reckoned a maverick in his diocese.)

When Pope John XXIII, in response to a sudden inspiration, decided to summon an ecumenical council, reactions throughout the world were often those of fear or even shock. "What do we need a council for?" "Why break up a winning team?" At the other extreme was anxiety lest a new council simply serve to freeze things more solidly than ever. Both "conservatives" and "progressives" were concerned that a council might get things "unstuck," or achieve no more than a few pious generalities followed by anathemas calculated to block tendencies labeled the "new theology."

Amid these dim hopes, what a breath of the Holy Spirit was felt when the Council issued its opening "Message to Humanity," which spoke with humility of the serious intention "of renewing ourselves and of becoming the ever more faithful witness of the Gospel of Christ." A fresh motif, this, in conciliar pronouncements. The message went on:

"We will devote ourselves with all our energy, with all our thoughts, toward renewing ourselves and the faithful entrusted to us." Not a vestige of triumph here; no trace of defensiveness, so usual during the previous state of siege. Instead, a willingness to face up honestly and courageously to reality, to renew, to change wherever change was called for. The date of this message, October 20, 1962, will surely be remembered as a turning point in recent Church history.

It was more than a year later, at the end of the first two sessions of the Council, December 4, 1963, that the next official document appeared. This was the Constitution on the Sacred Liturgy. Its opening paragraph continued the tone set by the Council's first message:

> This sacred Council has several aims in view: it desires to impart an ever increasing vigor to the Christian life of the faithful; *to adapt more suitably to the needs of our own times those institutions which are subject to change;* to foster whatever can promote union among all who believe in Christ; to strengthen whatever can help to call the whole of mankind into the household of the Church. The Council therefore sees particularly cogent reasons for undertaking the *reform* and promotion of the liturgy. [Italics added.]

The emphasized words show frankly the Church's acceptance of reform as a principle. That is to say, change is one of the very themes of the Council. Article 21 of the Constitution develops this theme:

> For the liturgy is made up of unchangeable elements divinely instituted and of *elements subject to change. These not only may but ought to be changed with the passage of time* if they have suffered from the intrusion of anything out of harmony with the inner nature of

24

the liturgy or *have become unsuited* to it. [Italics added.]

This clear distinction between "unchangeable elements divinely instituted" and "elements subject to change" is meaningful, indeed basic. It is clearly implied that only those elements of the liturgy that are instituted by God cannot be changed; the rest, however hallowed by age or human tradition, can be changed by the Church since they were instituted by the Church. Further, they not only may but ought to be changed if some of them have become useless or even damaging "with the passage of time."

Shortly before the August, 1964, National Liturgical Week was held in St. Louis, Cardinal Ritter explained this fundamental notion with great force and clarity. "Through the years," the cardinal said, "there are bound to have been intrusions of things that are out of harmony with the spirit of the liturgy." Sometimes, too, as he said, certain points of Catholic teaching were emphasized that are less meaningful or pertinent at other periods. This happened through the zeal of various groups of the faithful, or of bishops, or even of "overzealous Popes," who wished some ceremony to be added. Some of these added ceremonies, today, no longer serve the purpose for which they were intended.[1]

Perhaps the key phrase, however, of the Constitution's explanation of change is "with the passage of time." It had long been habitual for Catholics trained along the older catechetical lines, or in the seminary thesis procedure, to look for precise, succinct, neatly formulated and easily memorized answers to questions. True, no one would dispute the importance of knowing that there are precisely seven sacraments. Yet the danger inherent in such pithy statements, for all their usefulness, is that they invariably sound more complete and definitive than they are. The fact, say, that St. Augustine or even certain later Doctors of the Church would not have given the same simple answer to the question "How many sacraments are there?" suggests that a great deal more must be said before the reply can be fruitfully understood. Much of the development of dogma is implied here.

Little wonder that in the last several decades, parallel to the liturgical renewal, a remarkable new approach to religious instruction has become widespread. This "new" (though really very old and traditional) kerygmatic movement has made its impact on the liturgy. Thus we find it richly incorporated into the Council's Constitution, as we shall see in our discussion of *kerygma*, and its meaning, in the next chapter.

But "the passage of time" has further implications in this whole matter of change and specifically of liturgical change. If the whole of sacred history has been the process of God's self-revelation to man, the divine pedagogy has also respected the particular condition of mankind at each moment of history. God did not speak to the patriarchs in exactly the same images or terms that he used when speaking to the prophets, nor to the earlier prophets as to the later ones. In the New Testament, our Lord did not reveal Himself or His teaching in an instant. His method was adapted to the grasp and needs of His disciples as He found them and educated them. It was progressive, pedagogical, what has been called "economical."

Still less has man's response, in the Old and New Testaments, been identical at all periods. Worship is to a large extent a human function conditioned by human modes of imagining, understanding, living. Even if not a single "intrusion" had ever taken place—suppose, for a moment, that our Roman rite had indeed remained exactly as it was in the days of St. Augustine or St. Gregory, with no "intrusions" whatever—this would not exclude the possibility of change or the need for it.

The problem is not simply to rediscover antiquity (as Pope Pius XII warned in his great liturgical encyclical *Mediator Dei*), as though a single moment of the past could be chosen as an absolute, timeless, static ideal. For, in theologian Charles Davis' words, the Christian life is not "a timeless relationship with God." [2] There is a flow about everything that lives, and while not every change is healthful (witness cancer), to stop changing is to stop living, as we know life on earth. Change, as Cardinal Cushing told the faithful of his archdiocese, "is intrinsic to the renewal the Church is seeking." [3]

This human need for change—organic, vital change—is rooted in reality. Whatever interpretation we offer for the data of evolution, whether crudely mechanistic or in the more refined vision of Teilhard de Chardin, we cannot gainsay the fact that life is a dynamic, not a static, phenomenon. And while the more complex evolution of social organisms can hardly be interpreted in exactly the same terms as that of living organisms in the biological sense, anthropologists point to something in societies akin to human growth, maturity, and decay. Those societies that refuse to adapt to changing environments or new challenges become disrupted or even engulfed and absorbed by more organic cultures. Any process of learning involves change, both the learning done by individuals and that done by whole societies. As Chesterton put it, paradoxically, "If you leave a thing alone you leave it to a torrent of change; a white post soon becomes a black post."

Thus, while change may be dangerous, much as living is dangerous, refusal to change can be fatal. Faced with a changed environment and failing to adapt to it, an organism quickly becomes extinct. And just as our legacy of prehistory is rich in the fossilized remains of nonadapting animals, human history is full of the ruins of civilizations that allowed themselves to be bypassed by time.

The eminent sociologist and official expert at Vatican Council II, Father François Houtart, studies this point in depth in his work *The Challenge to Change,*[4] which merits careful reading by anyone interested in liturgical as well as other social changes. He explains that "perhaps the single most important value in a changing society is a capacity for *adaptation."* Then he goes on to show that awareness of this fact is "very important for the Church because the Church will be seen as something valuable in the world today if she accepts the possibility of adaptation, and the necessity for continual revision of her work and institutions."

Another important sociological study, *Vatican II: Last of the Councils,* by Jesuit Father Rock Caporale,[5] goes deeply into the question of change in the Church, especially as found in the work of the Council. The Council itself is an instrument of change and for change. Too, the present moment of history makes it evident that the Council needs further instruments to ensure the ongoing process of reform— what Father Caporale calls "the institutionalization of change itself." This in turn calls for a "theoretical justification of what has, as a matter of fact, taken place in history." For the Church has periodically undertaken the work of "adapting herself to varying situations and social conditions." This, as the Church has learned, has "proved healthful and useful for the achievement of her goals."

This stress on change and its acceptance by Catholic thinkers has been designated by another Council expert, Father Daniel J. O'Hanlon, as the very first trait in Catholic theology today.[6] Yet, though it was stressed a century ago in the work of several giant theologians like Möhler, Scheeben and notably Cardinal Newman, it has not until quite recently been studied in theology manuals. Newman's *Essay on the Development of Christian Doctrine* might, in fact, almost be described as an analysis of change as a mark of the Church. He finds the Church (indeed, this was a great factor in his conversion) "progressive," "ever germinating," rich in "sudden and wonderful changes," in "consolidations and adaptations." In the 1878 edition of the *Essay,* Newman goes so far as to enunciate this principle, which can bear repeated and long meditation: "In a higher world it is otherwise, but here below to live is to change, and to be perfect is to have changed often."

When it comes to worship, however, resistance to change assumes a tonality over and above the normal human preference for the unchanging and familiar. As we know, religion throughout history has been a sturdy cultural prop. In our style or way of encountering God, something within us seems to call for a degree of tradition and stylization. Father Aelred Baker, the English theologian, carefully phrases it thus: "All religions have fastened on God as the great conserver: whether in the simple form of a God always present amid the vicissitudes of human life or in the more sophisticated conception of a timeless world or eternity where God dwells outside the world of change in which we live." Then, quite predictably, there "arises the habit of seeing what is constant as religious and of presuming that what is religious ought to be constant." [7]

Father Baker goes on to remind us that "the Christian religion is probably the only one that has deliberately set out to be popular." Thus by the end of the fourth century sophisticated Latin writers found it a matter of shame and disgrace that even barbarians laid hands on the sacred text (not altogether unlike the resentment against some twentieth-century versions). Yet, as Father Baker finds, there remains something permanent about "the cautious way a man approaches God. He does not find it easy, and the liturgies of the world are proof enough that men readily adapt archaic and repetitive formulas to even their most personal approaches." This awareness should make us somewhat hesitant to condemn every symptom of conservatism since at least some of it seems endemic in the human religious attitude. It serves as a built-in brake on change, even when change is most imperative.

Why the special urgency in regard to change today? Several answers immediately come to mind. One is the particular moment of history in which we find ourselves: at the end of the "state of siege" that followed the upheavals of the sixteenth century, and even more the period of Enlightenment and revolution. The particular line of defense in use for some centuries was drawn up by apologists and polemicists and built on the Church's fundamental unchangeableness, her fidelity to the mission of "preserving all things." In the foregoing, one might read "conserving" for "preserving" for, as officially commissioned guardian of the deposit of faith, the Church understandably needs to be in many ways conservative. Whenever structures have seemed to be coming apart, an adhesive counteraction has been called for. Theologians who left the Church were promptly labeled "innovators," as the orthodox position was defensively held to as firmly as possible.

In the liturgy, lines were drawn up strictly. Where Protestantism stressed the universal priesthood of all Christians, Catholic apologists counterstressed the special priesthood of the ordained, saying little about the fact that Scripture speaks of the priestly people. Sometimes matters Catholic in themselves and deeply grounded in tradition (like the use of the vernacular tongues, or communion under both kinds, or the special liturgical meaning of the Word of God), having become fervently espoused by various Protestant groups, now became either neglected as smacking of heresy or, in certain cases, were utterly rejected from the liturgy. Had they not been taken as badges or shibboleths of heterodoxy, there is no reason to think they would not gradually have made their way back into the Catholic liturgy, with no uproar, long before Vatican Council II. This will be treated again in Chapter Six, "Liturgy and Ecumenism."

Further, certain very real abuses had crept into the liturgical practice of the faithful, especially during the later Middle Ages. Bizarre forms of devotion to the Elevation at Mass are mentioned by liturgical historians like Jungmann—such customs, among them, as urging the priest to prolong the Elevation in the belief that one did not age while gazing at the Host, or that the souls mentioned by name during the Elevation would receive certain and instant release from Purgatory.

The variety of rites from place to place also led to quite a few eccentricities. For example, of the hundreds of Prefaces used in different cities, not all were equally admirable. Möhlberg mentions one very picturesque Preface from Verona against monks who swindle widows out of their fortunes.[8] Small wonder that when the Roman Missal was reformed under St. Pius V (1570), a fairly strong position was taken against variety.

Seventeen years later, Pope Sixtus V set up a Congregation of Rites to keep close watch over any deviations from the fixed norm. While the rubrics laid down in the sixteenth century were far from frivolous, and certainly represented an improvement over the uneven and sometimes chaotic practices of the period just preceding the Reformation, they could hardly be expected to be permanently normative or satisfactory. For one thing, they were drawn up at a time when the historical studies of liturgical development had not even begun. For another, given the times, they were drawn up defensively and were inescapably conditioned by the climate of Reformation and Counter Reformation, a climate, it might be said, of more heat than light.

Yet, even if these rubrics had proved ideal for the period in which they were established, it does not follow that a century later they would have served the liturgical needs of the Church. And still less four centuries later.

Another reason why change is peculiarly urgent today, in liturgy as in other human elements of the Church's work, is the unprecedented acceleration of change in the world as a whole. Indeed, change may well be the most characteristic trait of our time. Take population, where the term "explosion" has become commonplace to describe this phase of change. In 1750, according to demographers, the annual increase in world population was about 3.7 million; today it is over 45 million. In 1830 the maximum speed was about twelve miles an hour; today, air travel is near the speed of sound, and space travel at least twenty times greater than that. As François Houtart observes, "We are reaching the point of living in a rapidly and perpetually *changing* society, and most probably this will continue until the end of the world."

If the Church is reluctant to change in those areas in which she is permitted to change, the lag between civilization and the Church's work on earth will continue to increase at a stupefying pace. And this would make her role seem ever more irrelevant.

Many persons, both Catholics and others, were not a little disappointed when the Council's first constitution proved to be one on the liturgy. They had hoped for something more obviously exciting, something, say, on birth control. Several reasons account for the liturgical document's coming first. One is its immediate impact on the whole Church. Another is the fact that much of the preliminary work had already been done.

Not only was liturgical reform well under way—thanks to the sixty-year-old "Liturgical Movement" and to Pius XII's superb encyclical on the Mystical Body (*Mystici Corporis,* June 29, 1943) and the complementary one on the liturgy (*Mediator Dei,* November 20, 1947)—but liturgical change offered an area of renewal which would take immediate tangible effect at every level of the Church, lay as well as clerical. Since we learn by doing, it was plain that by experiencing change in our everyday life of worship we might all become better prepared to accept the further changes called for in other conciliar decisions. For, as Bacon shrewdly observed, you must change many things if you want to change one thing. Liturgical change was to be only the beginning; but it did establish the principle.

One of the leading figures in the Church today, Léon-Joseph Cardinal Suenens, described the Council as "an invitation to an examination of conscience, a matter of getting clear what is essential in the Church and what is only incidental, what must remain and what is dependent on the times and circumstances." He sees the Council's work as one of "sorting out," in many sectors of the Church's life and activity. In the matter of liturgical change, no less than in the area to which he was addressing himself explicitly, he pointed out that we need "to overcome inertia, routine and the spiritual or intellectual laziness which everywhere favor a policy of no change." [9]

During his momentous visit to Bombay on December 3, 1964, Pope Paul spoke these prophetic words: "The human race is undergoing profound changes and is groping for the guiding principle and the new forces which will lead it into the world of the future." There can be little doubt that certain of these "profound changes" must be undergone by the Church too, not least in her liturgy.

There appears a strange ambiguity in attitudes toward present-day liturgical changes. Sometimes we hear them praised (or attacked) because they are newfangled. Quite as often they are argued for on the grounds that they are really quite ancient, even "apostolic." Something must be said about these two viewpoints.

In the first place, Christianity (unlike "nature" religions and most of the non-Judaeo-Christian religions) is a strongly historic religion, centered on specific and unique events: the call of Abraham, Passover, the coming of Christ. There is nothing inevitable or cyclic about these divine interruptions into human history. They are single, free acts of God in time and space. They demand a special kind of acceptance, response, loyalty. They change world history and our personal histories, and they cannot be undone. Hence there is a note of irreversibility about the Christian commitment—not, of course, in the sense that we cannot personally reject God's self-revelation, but in the further sense that every divine step takes place in one direction, toward one goal. Therefore to be Christian is to be in a profound sense traditional.

However, to be traditional is not at all the same as to be a "traditionalist" (as some antiprogressive Catholics like to call themselves). For the "traditionalist" has a short memory:

he canonizes the immediate past without seeing it and the present in the larger perspective of the full tradition, which is never static but ebbs and flows. To return to the figure of "perspective": we need to move away, to achieve a measure of detachment from immediate surroundings, in order to know where we are. In much the same way, we need a wide version of sacred history to see what there is about the present or the immediate past that really matters, and what is simply limited, trivial and ephemeral.

The problem then arises: which moments of the past are relevant to the present, and which are only encumbrances? The answer is not easy. For to say simply "the older the better" is to deny any sense of progress or possible gain; to say "the newer the better" is to slip into the parochialism of the present and beg the question. One very simple answer, which serves as a sort of practical norm, is to accept whatever the Council decrees is best and let it go at that. But the problem is not merely one of obeying the Council, but of understanding its meaning. When Pope Paul pleaded for understanding he surely meant something quite different from blind acceptance.

No one, I believe, would suggest that we all ought to have Mass today in the original Aramaic on the grounds that it was the language our Lord used; or in Greek because it is the language in which we have it recorded in the New Testament; or in Hebrew, since at least some of the Passover ceremony must have been conducted in that ancient, holy tongue. Even the most fervent archaist or "traditionalist" would draw the line before that. But on what principle? Presumably because the Aramaic and Greek and even the Hebrew languages, however awesome and venerable, do not touch the core; they are only peripheral to the question of what *we* ought to do *now*. Thus some kind of judgment has to be made as to what is "traditional" and what is only "old." In the choice of a referent, we must make a value judgment.

In its long history the Church has constantly had to make choices. Does, for example, our legacy from the second century have more pertinence today than that of the seventeenth century? Both must be part of tradition (ecclesiastical tradition, that is), but we cannot draw from both simultaneously in the same matter. Only in the meaningless chronological sense can the seventeenth century be said to include the second. For there remain values, in liturgy as elsewhere in our emphases, that are present in one century and not equally so in another. One, to a degree at least, excludes the other.

Accordingly, students of the liturgy are never content to absolutize any single moment of the past. True, they study the past, using the most careful historical techniques. But when it comes to judging what is needed in the present, they must apply criteria that are more than historical. Their problem then becomes the more complex one: What, in the rich tradition of the Church, are the structures that best apply to the needs of the faithful today? For example, are candles and liturgical vestments to be dispensed with because we now have electricity and more functional garb than did the early Christians?

Change, then, calls for an evaluation of the past as well as of the present. While every moment of the past has something to teach, and the early Church for obvious reasons enjoys a privileged place as teacher, our responsibility is to the present and, to an extent, to the future. The final decision rests with the teaching Church, under the Pope and bishops, who will use every resource of historical, theological, liturgical and sociological knowledge that is available in making any decision.

In purely sociological terms, however, even apart from the

assured divine safeguards against total or disastrous error, the Church does not need to be as timid about change as do other organizations. For in the Church there is a systemic interconnection between the membership system and the belief system; [10] for a member is a *believer,* and belief assures loyalty and stability. Further, the Catholic Church, with its strong hierarchical principle, can afford to be freer in embracing change than churches with a more congregational structure. I was at first surprised, then on reflection much less so, when a prominent Protestant theologian recently told me: "We're much more tradition-bound than you Catholics."

What has been called liturgical change, or the liturgical renewal or reform, represents no single current of development. It now appears as a mighty tide resulting from the convergence of a number of movements common to our century, some of them flowing from quite distinct (sometimes even apparently opposing) sources. One is the nineteenth century's Solesmes Movement and its revival of Gregorian chant, which now seems so remote from the heart of the liturgical renewal. Yet it would be unfair to neglect or minimize, for example, the part played by what is often called the "Romantic" vision of the monks of Solesmes Abbey—pioneers like Dom Guéranger, Dom Pothier, Dom Mocquereau and others. True, today's liturgists tend to smile at some of their attitudes, their overriding preoccupation with restoring the Roman rite, and especially the grand inheritance of Gregorian chant. For there lurks the undeniable danger that by simply trying to relive the glamorous past, as viewed through rose-tinted lenses, one may suppose that he is seriously involved in renewal. As Father Daniel F. Berrigan says in his *Essays on the Church,* "One can always restore Gothic or plain chant, and conclude that he has achieved something of value. But such a work is taxidermist rather than creative."

Father Louis Bouyer, in Chapter Two of his classic work, *Liturgical Piety*,[11] devotes an incisive criticism to the Solesmes approach with its attempted flight to the Middle Ages. Yet neither he nor anyone professionally skilled in liturgical history would gainsay the seminal influence of these dedicated monks, even if the seed, here as so often elsewhere, has had to suffer a sort of mystical death before bringing forth unexpected and greater fruits.

Another current, more directly related to liturgy as it is understood today, flowed from the pastoral concern of St. Pius X. Apart from his motu proprio *Tra le sollecitudini* (November 22, 1903) on sacred music, which not only consecrated certain golden moments of the past but also included an important new stress on liturgical participation, the saintly pontiff often insisted on new, more active approaches to the Blessed Sacrament. His repeated exhortations to frequent communion are certainly a vital source of the liturgical renewal as we know it in our time.

It was during the pontificate of St. Pius that the energetic Belgian monk, Dom Lambert Beauduin, gave a particularly strong pastoral orientation to liturgy. No longer was the Church's worship to seem like a monkish preoccupation solely, or even primarily. The late Father Gerald Ellard, who died at almost the same time as Dom Beauduin, traces this pastoral and missiological focus of the movement in an important essay, "The First Fifty Years." [12] This trend, so pertinent to our times, will be treated at some length in the present book.

Two theological movements have also paralleled that of the liturgy: the biblical and the patristic. Indeed, their thrust has so often coincided with it that one is often hard put to discern in the work of a given theologian which facet is more sharply evident. When, for example, the names of world-famous theologians like Herwegen, Casel, Vonier, de Lubac, Daniélou, Spicq, Mersch and Cerfaux come to mind, it is not easy to pigeonhole them in one discipline more than another. Their impact on liturgy and liturgical thinking has been immeasurable.[13]

Both of these movements have often taken the form of what Father O'Hanlon calls the second trait of contemporary Catholic thought: the return to the sources.[14] Far from being romantic or narrowly archaeological, the work of these movements may be said to have *reached* backward, rather than *moved* backward. Their emphasis in renewal has been on the *new* rather than on the *re-*. The special freshness of our biblical and patristic sources has been brought to bear on the present liturgical renewal.

It may be useful to return at this point to the objection touched on earlier in this chapter. "Why do we have to go back to the early Church, as though the Holy Spirit had abandoned the Church somewhere along the way?"

Pope Pius XII, in his *Mediator Dei*,[15] when admitting the principle of change for the human elements of the liturgy, pointed out (in paragraph 50) that "it happens from time to time that pious practices, lost in the course of time, are again called into use, and again renewed." He further pressed us to avoid "two extreme attitudes with regard to the past: a blind attachment and a complete contempt." Indeed, it is hard to imagine Pope Pius XII entering a solemn pontifical function in the manner required by the sixth-century Roman ceremonial practice—on horseback.

One of the leading liturgical scholars of our century, Father H. A. Reinhold, cautioned against allowing the liturgy to seem "archaic dilettantism, sheer joy of novelty or esoteric faddism." [16] At the same time, neither he nor any other serious scholar would ever suggest that we cannot learn from the past. It is impossible to exaggerate the value of such profound historical works as those of Father Josef A. Jungmann, notably his vast compendium, *Missarum Solemnia: The Mass of the Roman Rite*.[17] Such works of scholarship have provided the underpinning presupposed in the several liturgical changes of the past decade. I have it on the authority of theologian Father Gerald Ellard that, during the reforms of his pontificate, Pope Pius XII kept a copy of Jungmann's work in his private room and consulted it constantly.

History, as is obvious, can do much to explain the meaning of the Roman rite as a whole and of all of its parts. It can show why and when, for example, the Prologue to St. John's Gospel was appended to the Mass. Our first evidence for its use, as a sort of concluding blessing of the Mass, goes back only as far as the mid-thirteenth century. As late as the latter half of the sixteenth century it was not of universal use, even in Rome itself. Once we know this, we are in a better position to determine whether it should be kept today. The same applies to almost every blessing, genuflection, ceremony, sacred object or prayer in the Mass or in other liturgical services.

The changes now being made, and those in the process of preparation, are viewed not in terms of their age but in terms of their present function or dysfunction. Specifically, what is uppermost in the minds of scholars assisting in the liturgical reform is the pastoral function of each ceremony and its use today for the people of God engaged in the worship of God. When these ceremonies are made simpler it is not merely to render simplicity an absolute virtue in itself. Rather it is to make sure that the basic meaning of a rite is uncluttered by ceremonies which may be beautiful or picturesque in themselves, but which, viewed in relation to a rite's meaning, have become encumbrances. The most eloquent and edifying prayer may become a distraction if it interferes with the clear, authentic flow of the Mass, just as an ornament, however charming, can deface the true beauty of a well-designed building.

At the same time, allowing for all the reservations just made, it is hard to escape seeing an advantage in approaching the sources of our liturgical rites. As the Fathers of the Church pointed out, a stream tends to be purer when closer to its origin. Even so, we are not emancipated from the duty of judgment. We still need to discover the classic moment when a given rite reaches maximum effectiveness. And again, since we are to make a prudential judgment about needs of the present and immediate future, we must judge which forms are best for worshipers of our time and those of tomorrow.

Inevitably some errors or less-than-perfect solutions will result. However, if the principle of change is accepted we have the means of correcting these "errors" as soon as they are detected. True, this involves inconvenience to liturgical publishers and priests, and some slight inconvenience to the laity as well. Nor is it desirable, given the wide range of talent found within the people of God, to have too many changes too frequently. Some stability is needed for group activity.

Studying the history of our recent liturgical changes, I have been repeatedly struck by the seriousness and scholarship that inspired them. By no means are they the whimsical creation of faddists or eccentrics. Indeed, the changes in the Mass that have come in consequence of the Constitution were, in fact, almost all foreseen by the Church's leading professional liturgical scholars. The liturgical congresses held at Maria Laach (1951), Sainte-Odile (1952) and Lugano (1953) evoked a series of resolutions which have been incorporated almost verbatim into the Constitution and subsequent changes.[18]

These congresses, and others like them, included the most respected liturgical scholars of the world, and the résumé of their recommendations to the Sacred Congregation of Rites represented an exceptional consensus of research and reflection. Thus, by the time Vatican Council II and its commissions went into the matter of liturgical reform, they had at their disposal the accumulated scholarship that is almost unprecedented in Church history. In point of fact, the delay in the reform of the Roman Breviary, which affects the lives of priests so deeply, is due precisely to the need for finishing the very same type of research that was accomplished for the Mass and most of the sacraments.

Yet another trend in recent Catholic thought with strong repercussions on the liturgy has, of course, been the renewal of social awareness. While this has roots in Pope Leo XIII's *Rerum Novarum* (1891) and in the social thought that led to this revolutionary encyclical, we see it growing more fully in our century as a result of Pius XI's *Quadragesimo Anno* (1931), Pius XII's *Mystici Corporis* (1943), and John XXIII's *Mater et Magistra* and *Pacem in Terris*. Pope Paul's appointment of the venerable Canon Cardijn, and of a Negro, to the college of cardinals may be interpreted as a canonization of the renewed social awareness of our time. And the identification of men like the late Father John LaFarge with both the social and liturgical movements is symbolic of their convergence.

No less immediately related is the recent clarification of catechetical and kerygmatic insights in the past few decades. For in the liturgical changes consecrated by the Council none has more instant impact on us all than the new approach to the Word.[19]

two

The Word

*A*rticle 6 of the Constitution on the Sacred Liturgy gives us a clear summary of what worship means. It is both a *proclamation* and an *accomplishment* or, more simply, a *word* and a *work*.

Everyone who assists at Mass or receives the sacraments knows, at least dimly and inchoately, that he is participating in an important work. He was taught from childhood that the Mass is a *work* of sacrifice and that in the sacraments Christ does another valuable *work*, that of giving us grace. But until recently, unless he was particularly well instructed (as happily many were in this Missal Age), the person was less aware of the *word* in liturgical life. Indeed, he had probably never heard the term *proclamation* in relation to the liturgy, and if he had he perhaps interpreted it as having Protestant overtones or, at best, as sounding remote and exotic.

Yet right after the introductory articles of the Constitution, when the Council begins to explain what the liturgy is all about, the individual is confronted with *proclamation*. This is not, of course, to say that proclamation has suddenly usurped the place of sacrament or sacrifice. True, a new emphasis is present. But the Council, like a good teacher, knows that what is already obvious needs less emphasis while what has been overlooked or quite ignored needs more emphasis. For some centuries now we have thought of the Mass in particular and liturgy in general as simply a matter of sacraments and sacrifice.[1] This alone represents a revolution from the days when they were thought to be mainly solemn religious ceremonies.

At the beginning of this century, when St. Pius X was urging frequent communion and the beginnings of liturgical participation, and when Dom Lambert Beauduin was stressing the need for a pastorally oriented liturgy, we note too the inauguration of a new catechetical movement in Munich and Vienna. Dr. Heinrich Stieglitz and other experienced catechists, after using traditional question-and-answer techniques in teaching the faith, opened up new approaches more in line with contemporary pedagogical psychology. Modern methods were evolved (text-development, "learning by doing," the intuitive method and others) in several centers in the German-speaking world, and somewhat later in France and elsewhere.

In 1936, Innsbruck's famous liturgist Father Josef A. Jungmann published a volume which, though not yet translated into English, has nevertheless had an incalculable influence on attitudes throughout the English-speaking world, indeed in the entire Christian world: *Die Frohbotschaft und unsere Glaubensverkündigung (The Glad Tidings and our Proclamation of the Faith)*. Father Jungmann stressed the imperative need for a deep revolution in our presentation of the faith. For centuries, preaching had largely been either quite neglected, reduced to a simplified restatement of theological theses, or given in terms of moral exhortation—and predominantly negative exhortation at that. Jungmann showed that the sense of "good news" (which, of course, is the literal meaning of gospel) tended to be obscured by a cloud of technicalities. What was needed, especially in a time when the Christian message had to compete with so many rival, opposing messages, was more of a sense of joyous, hopeful discovery: a true "proclamation."

For the past thirty years the term *proclamation,* and notably its Greek form, *kerygma,* has been dominant in many catechetical, liturgical and theological circles, especially in Central and Northern Europe. While *kerygma,* like many "in" words, is not easily pinned down to a precise definition, it may be described as a new focus on what is central and most meaningful in divine revelation.

Kerygma means the heralded message. It is derived from the Greek words *keryx* (herald) and *kerysso* (the verb "to herald or "to proclaim"). Biblical scholars point out that it is the term used to describe St. John the Baptist's activity as Christ's precursor (Matthew 3:1; Mark 1:4), of Christ's own ministry (Matthew 4:17 and 3:1 and in the great command given by Christ to the apostles to "preach the Gospel to every creature" (Mark 16:15). The verb form is found 61 times in the New Testament and the noun seven times, especially in St. Paul, where it refers to the core of the Christian message.[2]

The "kerygmatic approach," then, gives a new focus to preaching and teaching, both within the liturgy and outside of it. It calls fresh attention to the preaching-teaching nucleus of Christian doctrine, drawing them pointedly toward the center, which is God's call to a new life in Christ. The kerygma is, thus, not so much a dogma or structure of dogmas, as it is a Person. Christ *is* the kerygma. He is the Good News. He is the Great Event of sacred history. This history unfolds in three phases: the preparatory or Old Testament (which St. Paul calls our "pedagogue" or tutor to Christ, Galatians 3:24); the achievement, or earthly life, death, resurrection and ascension of Christ; the consummation, which will take place as Christ appears in glory. Meantime, everything is geared to living the Christ-life. "I have come that they may have life" (John 10:10).

One could hardly take exception to the kerygmatic approach when it is presented in this way. Yet misunderstandings did arise. It was thought by some that stress on the proclamation might tend to minimize the demands of the Christian life or downplay the gains of theology and the development of doctrine. Accordingly, around the year 1950 a sharp controversy arose in regard to the kerygmatic movement.[3] Since then the air has cleared and the emphatically kerygmatic tone of the Constitution on the Sacred Liturgy, as well as many recent volumes on catechetics, show the real gains which are ours as a result of the kerygmatic movement.[4]

Still, something must be said about the two leading objections—as they were proposed some years ago and as they may recur—to the kerygmatic emphasis. One objection is that it seems to mark a retrograde movement, denying by implication the dogmatic enrichment of Christian thought since the apostles first proclaimed it. The other objection claims that, useful as the kerygma doubtless is in mission lands as a first heralding of the good news, it has little place in everyday liturgy and preaching.

In answer to the first objection, we may reflect again on the function of change. The change resulting from the kerygmatic approach is not made simply for the sake of change, or for the sake of archaism. If we return to the sources, it is because we find the water clearer there. To put it another way, if some lopping off is advocated, it is in order to restore the essential to its prominence, to reveal the core, to focus attention, which can otherwise be distracted or dissipated by sheer abundance of stimuli. It is very well for professional theologians to study all the niceties of sacramental causality, for instance, or the relations and processions of the Persons of the Blessed Trinity. For the Christian whose life must be sustained by the Word, it is more helpful to hear the Bible speak directly to him. The average Christian needs to hear the faith transmitted in the terms and symbols given us by the Holy Spirit in Holy Scripture. The Christian asks for bread and has a right to receive the bread of the Word.

The second objection overlooks the fact that evangelization, or the kerygma, has many grades. "It is a permanent part—a dimension if you like—of all preaching, one which is brought into play at every stage of the life of the Christian," [5] says the esteemed professor of the Gregorian University, Father Domenico Grasso. For, while the basic content of God's proclamation is always the same, the tone of its presentation, notably in the homily, will be constantly adjusted to the needs of the Christian community.

The homily, in today's liturgical context as distinguished from the type of sermon that most of us have been used to, marks another change in the liturgy. It is explicitly mentioned several times in the Constitution. Article 52 states that "the homily is to be highly esteemed as part of the liturgy itself." It further insists that at "those Masses which are celebrated with the assistance of the people on Sundays and holy days of obligation, it should not be omitted except for a serious reason." And earlier in the Constitution (Article 35.2), the homily is again called "part of the liturgical service." It "should draw its content mainly from scriptural and liturgical sources, and its character should be that of a proclamation of God's wonderful works in the history of salvation or in the mystery of Christ ever made present and active within us, especially in the celebration of the liturgy." We see here again the emphasis on proclamation or kerygma.

At the same time, one must grant that it is easier to say what a homily is *not* than what it *is*. Clearly it is not an interruption in the Mass; rather it is a part of it. Nor is it a service in competition with the proclamation of the Word—as though Epistle and Gospel were something to be gone through perfunctorily before settling down to the serious business of the important message, the sermon. Rather, the homily is a moment of concentration precisely on the Word of God as proclaimed, a moment in which the priest, together with the people, enters more fully into divine revelation.

At the famous catechetical Eichstätt Conference in Germany in 1960, in his talk "Basic Links Between Liturgy and Catechesis," Bishop Josef Blomjous (of Mwanza, Tanganyika) admirably expressed the function of the homily: "Not to convert non-Christians, nor to teach the truths of religion for the first time to Christians, but to instruct them in the faith which they already possess and to stimulate them in the morality which they practice already." Thus, the purpose of the homily "is to make more explicit the faith taught by the liturgy, and to exhort to the practice of Christian life for which the liturgy is a preparation and of which it is the most perfect expression." [6]

A good deal has been written recently about the homily. It is agreed that in it the speaker acts less in his own name than as the *leitourgos*, the very word St. Paul uses in Romans 4:16 to describe his priesthood of Christ. For in the liturgy the audience is no ordinary audience, or even a pious audience of good people, but the official assembly of the people of God. The spokesman acts in no more private a role than when he reads the Gospel or celebrates the rest of the Mass.

This is not to imply that in the homily the priest should be cold or impassive; rather, his words must be part of the proclamation. Thus, they must express the wonder of God's saving Word; they must have the true note of revelation; they must be burning, authentic, urgent. At the same time the priest should not adopt "the stained-glass voice," to use author Charles Merrill Smith's apt phrase.[7]

The distinguished liturgist Father Frank B. Norris recapitulates the ideal of the homily in his essay "Preaching the Word of God." [8] Father Norris points out that it should be an "opening-up" of the pertinent redemptive theme. Second, it must be relevant to the *particular* congregation, and not general, vague or dreamy. Third, it should show some connection with the sacramental action to follow, demonstrating the intimate link between Word and Sacrament. Cardinal Bea pointed out the link between Word and Sacrifice in his important speech at the Assisi Conference. He shows the great originality of the Mass, which from apostolic times combines "teaching" with the "breaking of the bread" (Acts 2:42).[9]

Both in the present changes and presumably in whatever further changes the foreseeable future will bring, the homily remains the most personal and precarious part of the liturgy —the one least hedged in by specific directives. So it is not surprising that the Constitution, in Articles 14–19, becomes most insistent on the liturgical formation of priests, both for those already ordained and still more for seminarians being prepared for the apostolate. "Pastors themselves, in the first place," should "become thoroughly imbued with the spirit and power of the liturgy." Professors of the liturgy "must be properly trained for their work in institutes which specialize in this subject." No longer, as has happened too often in the past, may liturgical instruction be a casual, hit-or-miss subsidiary course, directed by any professor who happened to care, or who simply happened to be free to handle the course. Quite realistically, the Constitution insists on an explicit formation in specialized institutes.

It requires no special powers of clairvoyance to see that this prescription of the Constitution will make all the difference. If it is conscientiously observed, and priests become thoroughly grounded in the liturgy, the liturgical renewal will sooner become a living reality. If not, and to the extent that it is not observed, there is little that can be expected from the Constitution.

This clerical formation is further spelled out. The study of sacred liturgy must be "ranked among the compulsory and major courses" in both seminaries and religious houses of study. In theological studies "it is to rank among the main courses." And other courses, too, must be taught in a way that will "clearly bring out the connection between their subjects and the liturgy, as also the unity which underlies all priestly training." For the priest is, first of all, the *leitourgos.*

The Constitution (in Article 17) shows deep understanding of yet another need in priestly training. If liturgical study is delayed until the seminarian has reached the formal course of theology, shortly before ordination, it will be too late. His personal attitudes will already be structured, and a mere course in liturgical theology will touch only the surface of his life and spirituality. Accordingly, seminarians and religious "shall be given a liturgical formation in their spiritual life . . . so that they may be able to understand the sacred rites and take part in them wholeheartedly." Again we are not dealing with mere speculative appreciation, for seminarians "will also need personally to celebrate the liturgical rites." Further, the liturgical spirit is not to be just something adventitious or ornamental. For "life in the seminaries and religious houses of study" is to be "thoroughly influenced by the spirit of the liturgy."

And finally, as though to preclude any possible evasion, the Constitution adds: "Priests, both secular and religious, who are already working in the Lord's vineyard are to be helped by every suitable means to understand ever more fully what it is that they are doing when they perform sacred rites; they are to be aided to live the liturgical life and to share it with the faithful entrusted to their care." Again the two-pronged stress on both theory and practice.[10]

Article 19 of the Constitution develops one of the central themes of the entire document: "With zeal and patience, pastors of souls must promote the liturgical instruction of the faithful, and also their active participation in the liturgy both internally and externally, taking into account their age and condition, their way of life, and standard of religious culture." So participation is not to be left to chance, but must be seriously fostered and explained. This participation is not to be superficial or primarily external or mechanical. Nor is it to be thought peripheral in the life of pastor or parish: "By so doing," states the Constitution emphatically about demonstration of this participation, "pastors will be fulfilling one of the chief duties of a faithful dispenser of the mysteries of God; and in this matter they must lead their flock not only in word but also by example."

The last possible excuse for postponement is thus sagaciously handled: the "we mustn't disturb people in their habits of devotion" mentality. Priests are instructed to lead with zeal as well as patience, by word as well as example, to help every soul to make the change from a less liturgical to a more liturgical spiritual life. The emphasis on example is possibly even more important than anything the priest might say. Everyone knows how in some parishes priests have undone the force of the Church's teaching on racial justice or other uncomfortable matters, by simply shrugging off the teaching even while stating it verbally.

The Council hopes to make the whole ministry of the Word fruitful, since it is the part of the liturgy that depends most on the priest's liturgical attitude and conviction. Whether or not St. Thomas was indulging in a rare hyperbole when he called preaching the "pre-eminent function of the priest," and whether the rite of ordination is doing the same when it names preaching in the first place among priestly duties, there can be no question of its importance—the cult of the Word, or, as has been said, "the cultic Word." Theologian Lambert Claussen puts it well in his essay on "The Mystery of Preaching": "To be an intermediary between God and man primarily involves announcing God's message and preaching Christ's Gospel to men."[11] Yet there still remains a mystery about preaching as part of the unfathomable mystery of priesthood itself.

Why should there be preaching? Ultimately because God has chosen to speak to man. Further, He speaks to man through men. Christ, through the Church, remaining with mankind to the very end of time, continually invites men to share in His prophetic function. And the official prophetic function is exercised through liturgical preaching, or what is called the homily.

In his stimulating work *Word and Revelation*,[12] Hans Urs von Balthasar probes deeply into the theology of the Word. As he illustrates, the Holy Scripture is quite unlike a tissue of Church definitions which aim mainly at putting an end to a period of uncertainty or solving a point of doubt or controversy. It rather "engenders a fresh perspective," or in Scheeben's words, "affords a fuller, deeper and more comprehensive understanding." As Urs von Balthasar sees it, since God's truth through Christ "is imparted to the soul in Scripture, no dialogue between God and the soul, however interior or mystical, ever takes precedence of Scripture or replaces it."

Still less, then, should the homily degenerate to the status of a merely human message. Just as the priest plays an instrumental role when he administers the sacraments (not coming *between* Christ and the Christian, but acting precisely *in the name* of Christ), so in the homily the priest speaks, as far as he is able, not in his own name but in that of Christ. The sermon, then, is no exercise in rhetoric or sacred eloquence, as though the spokesman were aspiring to be a latter-day Bossuet. (Coincidentally, Bossuet, for all his fame as an orator, has expressed the priest's role in words that can hardly be improved upon: "The preachers of the Gospel ascend the pulpit in the same spirit in which they approach the altar. They ascend to celebrate a mystery, a mystery very similar to the Eucharist. For the Body of Jesus Christ is no more truly contained in the adorable Sacrament than is the Truth of Jesus Christ in the preaching of the Gospel.") [13]

It is plain that preparation in homiletics will involve far more than academic proficiency. The priest, it is true, should, ideally, be as well versed in Holy Scripture and salvation history as he is in dogmatic theology. But if his formation is no more than intellectual it can hardly result in the style of homiletic preaching envisioned by the Council. For to preach using the methods of formal theology would be something like "taking chemists for cooks," as Newman put it. The Word must be lived in order to be offered as the living Word.

Hence the need for an ever deepening spiritual life in those who are to utter the Word today as well as in those who are to receive the Word. Romano Guardini's ever pertinent *Meditations Before Mass* [14] makes a good deal of the importance of silence as a preparation for the Word, both before and during the celebration—"that silence which establishes itself again and again during the ceremony." For "silence opens the inner fount from which the Word rises." True, to a large extent the liturgy consists of "words which we address to and receive from God." Yet "they must not degenerate to mere talk, which is the fate of all words, even the profoundest and holiest, when they are spoken improperly." At the same time, in Guardini's view, this silence must not be conceived as something negative, a gap or lacuna. "Actually it is something rich and brimming; it is a collected, total presence, a being 'all there,' receptive, alert, ready."

The Constitution makes the same point. In Article 12 it reminds us that "the Christian is indeed called to pray with his brethren, but he must also enter into his chamber to pray to the Father in secret." This caution is peculiarly relevant to the present phase of the liturgical movement. In our eagerness for participation and a community sense, some of us have at times given the impression that liturgy is only made up of a great deal of sound and fury, incessant singing and much fussy bustling and bobbing up and down.

How this new emphasis and understanding can best be propagated will depend on time and place. In religious communities, where life is geared to a measure of contemplation, it is more easily handled. In families, where children have to be washed and dressed and transported, the holy silence required if we are to hear the Word will seem a utopian ideal. Perhaps on the evening before a Mass or ceremony, or in the car on the way to church, mother or father could explain the meaning of what is to come, using the fine introductions to Sundays or feast days as given in the Fulton J. Sheen Sunday Missal, The Layman's Missal, the Bible Missal, the Maryknoll Missal, or the St. Andrew's Missal. These, in fact, present so much good material that it will be just a matter of choosing. And each gives just enough introduction while taking away nothing of the freshness of the liturgical proclamation itself.

Some short time should be allowed for immediate preparation before Mass, during which one becomes attuned, receptive, eager. We all know the immense difference between arriving at a game, concert or play at the last possible moment and arriving several minutes ahead of time. Arriving late allows no time for tuning oneself up to the event. Arriving early permits the sense of expectancy to build to a peak. Any symphony-goer knows the unique excitement provided by the gentle cacophony of an orchestra tuning up just before the concert. He knows the heightened, almost religious hush just as the conductor appears and again when he raises his baton. Since we are creatures of time, we need such moments of silence and anticipation if we are to appreciate anything important.

As long as parish Masses are scheduled rigidly "on the hour," the time one requires to prepare himself for the liturgical experience is limited. Traffic jams and the delays they cause are the least factor; more important is the lack of time to devote to the holy inner stillness that ought to precede the holy celebration. (And in Chapter Five we will discuss the parish's social sense that also is endangered if no time is allowed for people to gather at the end of a service.) The tyranny of the sixty-minute hour, as though it were of divine institution, is something from which all parishes should become emancipated as quickly as possible.[15]

Both priests and people need to take account of the special role of *listening* in our highly literate, visual and televisual age. It has been seriously asked whether today there is any need, or even the possibility, of the spoken word having any deep impact on us. "Why bother with all this, when I have my missal and can read for myself?" is one formulation of the question. Granted the changes in communication being brought about by twentieth-century media like radio and television.[16] Yet the effectiveness of orators even on sophisticated audiences seems little diminished today. Much of the power of Presidents Kennedy and Johnson had to do with their persuasive manner of using the spoken word, and anyone who has ever heard Dr. Martin Luther King is aware of the same power that has always moved men. The problem today is, rather, one of how to meet the competing standards of the media. Priests must read the Word and communicate the Word in the homily with greater conviction, sincerity and authentic passion than ever before.

Another of the major changes in the liturgy which has evoked strong responses, favorable or otherwise, is the wider use of the vernacular. Article 36 of the Constitution approached the language problem cautiously, with an obvious concession to anti-vernacularists. "Particular law remaining in force, the use of the Latin language is to be preserved in the Latin rites."

Having said this, the Constitution goes on: "But since the use of the mother tongue, whether in the Mass, the administration of the sacraments, or other parts of the liturgy, frequently may be of great advantage to the people, the limits of its employment may be extended." In the context of previous Roman legislation, which had always been most reluctant about any use of the "mother tongue" in the Latin rites (the Roman, Milanese and a few others of limited extent), this sentence, cautiously as it is worded, is one of the most far-reaching of the entire Constitution. It goes on to extend the use of the vernacular not only to the sacred readings, but to certain prayers and chants. Further specifications are set down in the remainder of Article 36, in Articles 54 (on "the common prayer"), 63 (the sacraments), 76 (ordination), 78 (the nuptial Mass), and 101 (the divine office). The range of use of the vernacular depends on the local bishops (Article 36.3), whose decrees are to be confirmed by the Holy See. Thus it is by no means a minor matter.

The case for the vernacular is one that has been widely discussed in recent years.[17] Briefly, the case may be summed up as follows: Language provides both a vehicle of communication and a structure of thought. Both functions are normally best accomplished in one's mother tongue. While there is no question in Catholic theology that the Mass and sacraments are *validly* served by a foreign language—Latin or some other—it seems clear that the needs of the faithful (and of the priest, too) are better cared for in their own language. Other values are not meant to be downgraded: the symbolism of unity (at least within countries where the Latin rites are predominant); and the sense of dignity and mystery. Yet, on reflection, it seems that these values can be adequately upheld by means other than the use of Latin: for example, by having the liturgy's content better understood and shared in (thus, even when attending a church far away from home one really understands what the priest is saying just as he understood it fully in his parish church);

by the effective use of music and the visual arts; and by making use of the rich world of symbolism. (We will explore this symbolism in the next chapter.)

I see no cogent reason, apart from obedience to regulations, for the present oscillation between the vernacular and Latin. Instead of serving to keep Latin in some sort of primacy, experience shows that the effort is generally quite the opposite. Priests and laity in all parts of the country with whom I have discussed this are almost unanimously dissatisfied with the present "hybrid" or "macaronic" effect produced by the current circumstances. They feel that the effect only heightens the opacity of Latin and its failure as a language for the great majority of Americans. Some go so far as to say: "Either all English, or even a return to all Latin; anything rather than this." I, personally, do not go so far. I would rather have the present halfway measure than all Latin, since the central function of serving the Word is at least partly carried out.

At the risk of indelicacy, I wish to assure readers that I have no personal antipathy toward Latin. Thanks to postgraduate studies, largely under the great medievalist Father Otto J. Kuhnmuench, and again at Oxford, and to many years of teaching in seminaries and colleges, I find much Latin literature a great delight and even a source of relaxation and recreation. The lapidary majesty of the Roman canon and many of the older collects, as well as the unction of the *Te Deum* and many passages of the Latin Fathers, are treasures with which many professional classical scholars cannot part except with a great sense of personal loss. (I might also mention the perfection of the Ambrosian and certain other hymns—by no means all, however: any Latinist regrets the revisions of hymns carried on in the sixteenth century in the name of classicism.)

58

Nonetheless, it is hard to escape the persuasion that a totally vernacular liturgy is desirable for almost all the faithful and for most priests. For the time being, some option might well be allowed—an early Mass in "traditional" manner, for instance—for people who find it excessively hard to change. And in the matter of the divine office, when it is said privately (and at least until the full reform takes place), I personally prefer the freedom to use either Latin or the vernacular.

At the same time, all upholders of the vernacular position have repeatedly insisted that the vernacular is no panacea. Indeed, it raises new (though foreseen) problems which now have to be faced. In particular, there is the matter of which vernacular is to be used.[18]

The present English version used in the United States is not yet satisfactory in the opinion of most critics. At the same time, it is not wholly appalling to them. A strong case can be made for the new version used at Mass for the Epistles and Gospels (taken from the new Confraternity translation of the New Testament). One of the translators, Father Raymond E. Brown, has presented a defense in his article, "Our New Translation of the Bible," appearing in the November 14, 1964, issue of *America*.

True, the new version does not read aloud with the easy, comfortable rhythm that we have been used to. Yet most of us who have taken the trouble to prepare our oral reading have found that it manages to be both intelligible and timely. One may cavil at a word choice here and there; but it is well to remember that these words were selected by a group of trained Scripture scholars whose sense of the nuances of each original Greek word can be presumed to be more accurate than that of anyone not a specialist. Further, we should not discount the "shock" value of a translation that is meant to reflect the very Word of God given in the language of the apostles and evangelists, whose styles are frequently quite personal and jagged and by no means as flowing as that of Plato or as sonorous as that of the King James version.

At the same time, one needs to keep in mind that words are the most delicate of signs, the most perishable of counters, the most elusive of tokens. To put it more prosaically, words are not the simple, transparent, unambiguous things they seem. They are clouded or enriched by use, context, denotation, and they possess a stark connotation. Like the human beings whose instruments they are, words have a history, individually and collectively. The magic of a Shakespeare, a Joyce, a Yeats is not a common inheritance to be called up at will. And interpretive talent is required if one is to enter their linguistic worlds with any sensitivity whatever.[19]

The great art historian and critic E. H. Gombrich has penetrated deeply into these and related problems in several published volumes as well as in a recent article, "The Use of Art for the Study of Symbols." [20] He notes that in poetry as in other arts, and to a considerable extent in prose of high quality, the several elements do not make a simple impact in simple sequence. Often they are "telescoped and condensed into one" and the "effect of this simultaneity can be dramatic."

Thus, when scholars like G. B. Harrison or masters of the craft of writing like Evelyn Waugh plead with our translators to show some respect for language, they are not being merely precious or prissy. Anyone who has struggled to turn into English, say, something of the rich flavor of *Tantum ergo Sacramentum,* knows what a line of obstacles he faces. And who but a master poet could possibly evoke the terror of *Tuba mirum spargens sonum* in four equally shattering trochees? Truly, the translator's lot is not a happy one.

All the more reason for us to secure writers of high craftsmanship before our translations of the liturgy, or new prayers added to it, are committed to anything like a permanent form. Even if it is unhappily true that prose masters like Cranmer are not born every day or even every decade, our conclusion should not be that all is lost. Rather, it should be that we have a duty to look long and hard. Such an important service to the Word of God and the people of God should not be entrusted to unprofessional writers whose talent may be limited to great good will and a fondness for the liturgy. Even the sincerest love, unaided, cannot make a poem or even a line of worthy prose. As C. S. Lewis points out in his *Letters to Malcolm,* there is a special literary talent needed for composing a good prayer. "Prayer needs to be not only very good but very good in a very special way, if it is to stand up to reiterated reading aloud." It is sad that C. S. Lewis died before he could be invited to give us the kind of English translation we need, and that Evelyn Waugh refuses to accept a possible invitation. But surely there are others, like W. H. Auden, David Jones and Thomas Merton, to name a few.

Another problem about translation has been clearly stated by C. S. Lewis in the same volume. "If you have a vernacular liturgy you must have a changing liturgy: otherwise it will finally be vernacular only in name. The ideal of 'timeless English' is sheer nonsense. No living language can be timeless. You might as well ask for a motionless river." Whether or not Mr. Lewis was intending to castigate Ronald Knox's ideal of "timeless English" (brilliantly, if not altogether convincingly defended in his exquisite little book *Trials of a Translator*), he seems to have a point. At the same time,

he is speaking as an Anglican in favor of the Anglican service and against what he calls the "liturgical fidget." Most
of us who have witnessed the Anglican liturgy, or who
watched the Churchill funeral on television, would happily
trade our linguistic situation for this.

In any case, Mr. Lewis' distaste for a changing vernacular
liturgy, while easy to understand, seems to be too little
related to our own pressing need for a *pastoral* liturgy. Nor
does vernacular have to be restricted to the latest cant or
journalese. Yet it is useful for us to discover that even
the Anglicans, with roughly four centuries of experience,
still face a language problem. This situation suggests that
it is quite utopian to advise waiting until everything is
perfect before we risk doing anything.

One foreseeable by-product of the new use of the vernacular has been to reveal the many inadequacies of our present
liturgical prayers. Anyone who has conducted a funeral using
the new translations must have been distressed not only at
the quality of the English, but at much of the content, too.
Father A. Gregory Murray, one of our pioneer vernacularists,
expressed this in a letter to the London *Tablet* on January
9, 1965: "I hope we shall soon be permitted to omit the
Dies Irae at funeral Masses. Thank God, it still remains in
Latin [he is speaking of England; we are not so fortunate
in America], for, however much we may admire it, it strikes
a discordant note in what is otherwise a serene Mass of
pleading for God's mercy. Could not this much-too-long
sequence be returned to its original place—as a hymn in
connection with the Last Judgment Gospel of Advent Sunday? It had no place originally in Masses for the dead."

Regarding the hymns of the breviary, too, I go along with
Father Clifford Howell when he suggests that "the only real
solution is to scrap those Latin hymns and replace them with

hymns originally composed in English by English poets." [21]
I should, in fact, be inclined to push the solution even further
and do away with obligatory hymns in private recitation
of the breviary, since in such private recitation few of us
do any singing. I see nothing, however, against the possibility of including sacred poetry to be *read,* though I shudder
at the prospect of having to submit to choices dictated by
officialdom. The charism of infallibility does not seem to
extend to literary sensibility.

Something should be said in this chapter about the stress
on the kerygma that runs through a later document promulgated at Vatican Council II—indeed, its most impressive
statement to date—the Constitution on the Church. [This
is being written at the start of the fourth session, from which
much is expected.] Far from being a textbookish, seminary-
manual, juridically oriented pronouncement, the new Constitution on the Church breathes the very spirit of the
kerygma and the liturgy as presented in the earlier Constitution.

Its opening sentence illustrates this: "Christ is the Light
of the nations." It then goes on to speak of "proclaiming
the Gospel to every creature," using the very word—proclaiming—from which the term kerygma is derived (Mark
16:15).

Chapter I of the Constitution, titled "The Mystery of the
Church," restates the kerygma in terms adapted to the present day. The word "mystery," as well as the stress on mystery, is the key used by St. Paul to open God's eternal plan,
which is the very core of the kerygma (1 Cor. 2:1; Eph. 1:9
and 3:9; Rom. 16:25; and elsewhere).

The same chapter goes on to quote or paraphrase scrip-
tual text after text, theme after theme, unfolding the mystery

of salvation (Col. 1:15; Eph. 1:4–5 and 2:18; Rom. 8:10–11; Gal. 4:6; 1 Cor. 5:7 and 10:17; and further). The early Fathers of the Church, too, whose teaching is altogether impregnated with the kerygmatic, are quoted or alluded to, and in the notes to the text of the Constitution we find a tissue of patristic tradition. This illustrates a point made in the previous chapter about the three vital currents of contemporary Catholic thought and the way they flow together: the scriptural, the patristic, and the liturgical.

Article 6 of the Constitution on the Church is particularly enlightening: "In the Old Testament the revelation of the Kingdom is often conveyed by means of metaphors. In the same way the inner nature of the Church is now made known to us in different images taken either from tending sheep or cultivating the land, from building or from family life and betrothals; the images receive preparatory shaping in the books of the Prophets." The article goes on to instance some of these figures: "The Church is a *sheepfold*, whose one and indispensable *door* is Christ. It is a *flock* of which God Himself foretold He would be the *shepherd*, and whose *sheep*, though ruled by human *shepherds*, are nevertheless continuously led and nourished by Christ Himself, the Good Shepherd and the Prince of the shepherds, Who gave His life for the sheep." The Church is also called "a *piece of land* to be cultivated" (1 Cor. 3:9); the "choice *vineyard*" (Matthew 21, alluding to Isaiah 5); the "*building* of God," with Christ the *Cornerstone*; the "*house* of God in which His *family* dwells"; "the holy *temple*"; "the *New Jerusalem*"; "the *bride*"; "our *mother*"; "the spotless *spouse* of the spotless *Lamb*"; and so forth.

All of these diverse figures of speech, drawn from Holy Scripture and lovingly developed by the Fathers of the Church, present a many-faceted vision of the Church. Each adds some enriching insight, which also serves as a corrective to any oversimplified formula. Taken together, they save us from caricaturing the Church as a rigid, however sacred, power structure or monolithic juridical entity. They also offer a countervalent stream of emphases even against the organic but limited metaphor of the Mystical Body; for, fruitful as this has proved in our century (it is, moreover, treated in Article 7), it by no means exhausts the full mystery of the Church, and is only a part, not the whole, of the kerygma.

Karl Rahner points to the danger of our shrinking the Christian message by neglect of certain areas. "We may sometimes get the impression nowadays," he wrote before the Council began, "that there are truths in the Church which, although they are not indeed disputed in their explicit formulation, are being silenced to death by the fact that no one takes any notice of them any longer in the practice of their religious life. They are to be found in the Catechism, but they are not inscribed 'in our hearts on tables of flesh.'" [22]

It is plainly the purpose of the Council—notably in the two great Constitutions on the Liturgy and on the Church—to redress the balance, to restore proportions, to situate and interrelate the central truths of divine revelation. Nor can the work ever be reckoned as done once and for all. Future councils (or whatever instrumentality the Church of the future may use) will continue the ongoing task until the Parousia—the Second Coming. [23]

Not the least of our present tasks is to restore the significance of God's Word in our life and worship. For, as the eminent theologian Otto Semmelroth has recently reminded us, the Word not only disposes the faithful to receive the sacraments more rewardingly, but it possesses a sanctifying power in itself. Just as the Incarnation and Christ's Sacrifice are complementary parts of the complete work of salvation, so, too, the Word—and preaching the Word, inasmuch as one's preaching is a faithful outpouring of the Word—and the sacraments are complementary aspects of the Church's work in communicating grace. "The ministry of the Word and the ministry of the sacraments are related to one another like the two phases of a dialogue." [24]

It is now time to examine the Council's new stress on sacramentalism.

THREE

Sacraments and Symbols

*W*hen we talk of sacraments, suggests Dom Anscar Vonier, one of our century's leading liturgical theologians, we can never insist enough on this: "Before all things and above all things we are dealing with signs and symbols." [1] This is a useful reminder since, while Catholic practice has for some time been strongly "sacramental," it has given the impression, paradoxical as it may seem, of downgrading symbolism. The paradox lies, of course, in the fact that sacrament means sign or symbol, even while meaning something much more.

Recent philosophy has been very much occupied with symbolism and it would be impossible to summarize even the principal works that have appeared on the subject.[2] Whatever definition we decide to use, it must include the element of pointing to something else.

Symbols, however, are more than signs. They are roomy. They involve manifoldness. They are describable, but never fully definable. The symbol, by packing so much into itself, "opens up a level of reality, of being and corresponding meaning, which otherwise we could not reach," as Father

Terrence Toland explains in his important essay "Christian Sacrament: Sign and Experience." [3]

The richness of true, natural, elemental symbols is present everywhere in the liturgy, however little Catholics have been aware of them in the last few centuries. For long our stress has been so largely focused on the efficacy of the sacraments, their *ex opere operato* effectiveness, that we have often allowd their further meaning to move into the penumbra of thought and experience. By concentrating on the Real Presence, for example, we have left comparatively unstressed the very significant command of our Lord to *eat*. And while beautiful and grace-filled devotions have grown out of the one emphasis, there has resulted some consequent loss. Indeed, for a number of centuries, the very devotion to the Blessed Sacrament as *adorable* went along with an excessive fear of approaching the holy table. It seems to have occurred to few spiritual writers that if Christ had intended the Eucharist to be principally a sacrament of presence-to-be-adored, He would more than likely have chosen a symbol more suggestive than that of bread and wine—a precious jewel, for instance, or a golden image. Instead, He chose the commonest everyday *food*.

Another instance of our impoverishment in sacramental life and devotion appears in the sacraments of initiation: Baptism and Confirmation.[4] When only the efficacy of Baptism was in view, much of the meaning of that wondrous sacrament was forgotten. True, Christians were meticulously instructed on the minimum requirements for validity: what kind of water, how much, and the like. Since only a few drops were all that was judged rigorously necessary, Baptism came to seem like a ceremony merely of washing, and only a very vestigial one at that. All the rich symbolism of water as stressed in Holy Scripture—including its images of life and death—was sacrificed on the altar of clarity and simplification. The fact that Baptism principally meant our plunging into the death and resurrection of Christ (as now stressed in the Constitution, Article 6) was almost entirely bypassed. Little wonder that the Constitution devotes five articles (66–70) to the need for a revision of the present rite of Baptism.

Happily, too, the Constitution directs that the rite of Confirmation be revised also, and "the intimate connection which this sacrament has with the whole process of Christian initiation is to be more clearly set forth" (Article 71). With regard to the symbolism of Confirmation, it is ironical that almost the only symbol, in fact just about the only event remembered by most people in Confirmation, is one where the meaning is taken as almost the very opposite of that intended: the "slap" given by the bishop is a vestige of the kiss which he imparted to the newly confirmed Christian, welcoming him as a new worker for Christ. It is not a "blow" at all.[5]

The Constitution does not provide a theological, much less a philosophical, disquisition on the meaning and role of symbolism in the liturgy. It takes this role for granted. Referring to the sacraments as signs, it quickly adds that "since they are signs they also instruct" (Article 59). They "nourish, strengthen and express" faith. "They have indeed the power to impart grace, but, in addition, the very act of celebrating them effectively disposes the faithful to receive this grace fruitfully, to worship God duly and to love each other mutually. It is therefore of the highest importance that the faithful should easily understand the sacramental signs." [6]

Anyone—and with no more than the old-fashioned catechetical knowledge of sacramental teaching—would probably be entirely bewildered by this new emphasis. It calls for an understanding of the symbolism if one is to receive the sacraments "fruitfully," and dwells on the sacraments as *worship,* as well as on their social consequences.

The Constitution then reiterates the important sacramental principle that "there is hardly any proper use of material things which cannot be directed towards the sanctification of men and the praise of God" (Article 61). There follows a sad admission that not all is well in our use of symbolism: "With the passage of time, however, there have crept into the rites of the sacraments and sacramentals certain features which have rendered their nature and purpose far from clear to the people of today; hence some changes have become necessary to adapt them to the needs of our own times."

Earlier in the Constitution the same principle had been enunciated: the fact that in the liturgy "the sanctification of man is signified by signs perceptible to the senses, and is effected in a way which corresponds with each of these signs" (Article 7). In another article (34), we were reminded, too, that "the rites should be distinguished by a noble simplicity," and that these rites should be "within the people's power of comprehension." Obviously—though the obviousness had somehow escaped many people for a long time—the symbolism and general ritual should not become too involved to be really functional. The Constitution adds: "Normally they should not require much explanation."

In our new approach to symbolism in the liturgy, it thus seems plain that we must be cautious not to fall between the two stools of angelism and aestheticism. Angelism, which interprets man as purely intellectual, tends toward making everything totally rational and intelligible and, in a sense, cold. A liturgy for angels would, if it existed at all, have no need for symbols. For angels, as theologians who have studied these deep matters tell us, are pure intellects who grasp everything intuitively and clearly. Man, however, is more complex, very much enmeshed in matter; and depth psychology has opened to us some of the interesting implications of our special human psychic structure. And so we find today's psychologists more interested in symbols than ever before.[7]

The other slippery stool, aestheticism, puts such stress on artistic interest as to minimize the values of clarity and simplicity. Recent art has happily reacted with vigor against the type of opulence that used to clutter our churches, and, in fact, our ceremonies and sacramental life generally. It is thus far removed from the aestheticism that often tended toward the proliferation and crude complication of symbols. The Council's praise of "noble simplicity" certainly rings a bell that most contemporary artists and architects find sympathetic.

The move toward clarifying the Mass's structure, by eliminating certain recent additions (like the Last Gospel and the Leonine prayers) and by clearly relating the priest's position to individual parts of the Mass (the ambo or chair for the Service of the Word, with the altar of sacrifice reserved to the strictly Eucharistic sacrifice-banquet), is a step toward a more functional symbolism. So is the reduction in the number of repeated gestures (the endless signs of the cross, for example, and the kisses given to ceremonial objects at a solemn Mass). No one doubts that the sign of the cross is an effective symbol, as indeed are certain cruciform images in our church buildings. But surfeit quickly becomes self-defeating, and riches are not always the same as enrichment.

Again, I do not mean to imply that "the fewer symbols the better" is the right axiomatic answer to "the more the better." Some adjustment needs to be made to different cultures, ages, traditions and levels of sophistication. A church

designed to serve as a university chapel, for instance, might
suitably be more austere and subtle in its symbolism than,
say, one for a more diversified parish. Obviously, too, some
problems arise with regard to the ceremonies surrounding
the core of the sacraments. Here the Constitution is careful
not to canonize rigidity as a norm: "The Church has no wish
to impose a rigid uniformity. . . . Rather she respects and
fosters the genius and talents of the various races and nations" (Article 37). In revising liturgical ceremonies, adaptations are to be made for "different groups, regions and
peoples" (Article 38). Further, since as everyone knows
certain symbols may even have opposing significance in
different cultures or at different epochs, care must be taken
here too. A familiar instance is the use of white garments
for mourning in contrast to the customary black. It is an
elementary principle of missiology that adaptations are often
needed, and the classic case of the "Chinese Rites" shows
what damage can be done even by zealous persons who use
unduly inflexible methods: Had certain Chinese ritual customs been allowed in the Christian liturgy, as requested by
many missioners, Christianity would not have seemed so
alien and unacceptable.

Certain symbols used in the liturgy are so nearly universal
in human experience—like the kiss of the book of gospels,
the bow, the upheld hands, changes of posture—that they
require little explanation and not much adaptation (except,
of course, where an individual culture may find them objectionable). A number, too, have become so very much a part
of our ritual habits as to seem natural in themselves: for
example, kneeling, bowing, and praying with folded hands.
No one in our culture would, I believe, object to their use.
At the same time, the symbolism of standing at communion
seems so appropriate (as a symbol of joy at our reception of

the Risen Christ) and so rooted in our older tradition, that one finds it hard to understand the violent opposition to this practice encountered in some quarters.

Yet even symbols that are almost universal—like water, bread, oil—are not univocal in their meaning. For example, water does not suggest the same thing to a farmer, a nomad in the desert, a sailor, a dweller in swampy areas, or a city dweller. Nor is wheat bread a universal phenomenon, or wine from grapes. Nor does oil play as important a role in our daily life (except, of course, the oil of lubrication) as it does in simpler societies. Nor is the liturgical kiss of peace quite natural between men in Anglo-Saxon lands. Thus, even a brief analysis shows that symbolism in the liturgy is far from uncomplicated, and the problem is by no means merely a missiological one. We need close study and a willingness to make adaptations perhaps further than is commonly supposed.[8]

It would be exceedingly naïve to conclude that our sophisticated age has no further need for symbolism. Think of the excitement engendered not long ago when it was revealed that a plot was under way to bomb the Statue of Liberty, the Washington Monument and the Liberty Bell; an assassination conspiracy against the President could hardly have been more resented. Yet the proposed bombing was only a symbolic way of degrading three national symbols.

The same may be said of many protest demonstrations—whether against segregated institutions in the South, or against the United States in far-flung capitals—which have become very much a part of our national and international experience. Our concern is not about restaurants or physically torn flags or a few splashes of ink. It goes to the meaning symbolized—something (at a somewhat shallower level) akin to the exuberance we all feel in relation to athletic contests, especially where student elation or depression has nothing to do with the quality of performance, but with the loyalties symbolized in "our" team.

In the realm of religion, symbolism is no less universal.[9] We find it in some form in all religions, since, as Father Herbert Musurillo describes it, it fills the human psyche with images, memories, attitudes that make the religious man different, "encoding or transforming psychic experience." St. Augustine goes so far as to call the sacraments "visible words," since they are part of the communication common to man; indeed, there is probably no religion without at least some analogue to sacraments; even the Quakers use the symbolic value of silence in their worship.

Hence, a liturgical attitude will not be reluctant to accept symbols, as though they were somehow less than adult. This is not to say that every symbol added to the liturgy throughout the centuries remains equally valid or relevant. But Christians especially, whose religion is centered on the Incarnation, can never find symbolism or sacramentalism alien, however much their specific forms may vary. Sacraments and sacramentals are a consequence of the Incarnation. Even scientifically speaking, they are, as the noted psychologist Father Vincent V. Herr says, "physical or visible signs that God is dealing in a special manner with men, reaching down to man, renewing His once-redemptive act ever anew." [10]

Yet even at the least mystical level, there is plainly a built-in human need for ritual, rite, ceremony. In Saint-Exupéry's fable, *The Little Prince,* we recall the passage where the sage Fox used the word *rite.* The Little Prince was puzzled when the Fox said: "We need rites." "What are rites?" he naturally asked. Replied the Fox, "Rites are things that make one day different from another."

Rites do make one day different from another, but they

do more than that. They serve to elevate the commonplace, not only by way of relief or escape, but by pointing to something more important. The Fourth of July is not only a holiday from work; it is a reminder of something higher than such a private value. At a political level, it fulfills a liturgical need, ceremonially lifting us from the drabness of day-to-day existence, assuring us at least annually of our inheritance and share in something more than a private possession or solipsistic value. For this purpose, any day would do; but a day symbolically associated with an important event in our national history does it more richly, at more levels. Flag Day does so too, but with its own accent, as does Memorial Day, again with a touch of seriousness that tends to inspire the citizen to make the sacrifices necessary for authentic citizenship. Mother's Day and its pale echo, Father's Day, are ceremonial moments for expressing something that should be expressed more often. Yet the fact that the whole nation does it turns them into something wider than the individual family ritual for birthdays and anniversaries.

This leads us to the section of the Constitution that has to do with the liturgical year and to another change of attitude expected by the Council. In the common understanding of Church seasons and feasts, as well as in the cycle of the saints, we have suffered from a certain lack of theological sophistication. For such annual events must not be lowered to the level of mere traditional observances, such as Washington's birthday or the other days mentioned. They are that, but they are much more.

The Constitution devotes Chapter 5 to the matter of the liturgical year. Article 107 assures us that "the liturgical year is to be revised" in such a way as to "nourish duly the piety of the faithful who celebrate the mysteries of Christian redemption, especially the paschal mystery." Article 108 develops this theme, insisting that we are to be directed "primarily toward the feasts of the Lord whereby the mysteries of salvation are celebrated." Thus, we must not allow any feast to seem more important than those of the great redemptive mysteries. Article III, while reminding us of the value of devotion to the saints—"they proclaim the wonderful works of Christ in His servants and display to the faithful fitting examples for their imitation"—calls for restrictions on the number of saints' festivals, in order precisely to stress "the feasts which commemorate the very mysteries of salvation."

Devotion to the saints, while it has taken on quite varied forms throughout the centuries, is profoundly rooted in Catholic tradition and will surely not be abandoned.[11] Nevertheless, during the Middle Ages local devotions and feasts became so multiplied that Sunday Masses were frequently displaced by them, and the proportion of the liturgical seasons somewhat distorted. With the liturgical reforms of the sixteenth century, many of these saints' days were removed from the liturgical calendar. Since then, however, the calendar has again become crowded with all manner of new feasts, as saint after saint has been canonized. Several recent reforms have attempted to re-establish the correct balance by reducing the number and rank of saints' feasts, but the Constitution opens the way toward a still more thoroughgoing reform.

It also proposes a remedial formula of feasts: "Many should be left to be celebrated by some particular church or nation or religious order" (Article III). This should satisfy local demands without enforcing the devotional needs of one area or all. This also fits into the general policy of admissible diversity, as enunciated in Article 37: "The Church

76

has no wish to impose a rigid uniformity in matters which do not implicate the faith or the good of the whole community."

The great focus of Chapter 5 is, of course, on the paschal mystery. Easter, as instructed Christians are aware, is no ordinary feast, or even the first among equals. It is the unique feast—indeed, in the early Church it was the only feast—to which other days are related. Our tradition of celebrating Sundays is, of course, derived from Easter (Article 106). Again and again throughout the chapter we read of the importance of Sunday—"the foundation and kernel of the whole liturgical year," "the original feast day," the day on which "Christ's faithful should come together into one place so that, by hearing the word and taking part in the Eucharist, they may call to mind the passion, resurrection and glorification of the Lord Jesus, and may thank God Who 'has begotten them again, through the resurrection of Jesus Christ from the dead, unto a living hope' (1 Peter 1:3)."

This passage is an echo of earlier key articles in the Constitution (5–8), which bear repeated reading and reflection. They deal with the paschal mystery and its Eucharistic celebration.[12]

This paschal-centered emphasis of the renewed liturgy must carry through to the sacraments and sacramentals in general, and notably to a healthy approach to eschatology—what is called the teaching on the "four last things." Most urgently needed, as we mentioned earlier, is a reform of the Christian burial service, which the Constitution insists "should express more clearly the paschal character of Christian death" (Article 81). This is, of course, in line with the richer understanding of the Christian kerygma and the fuller development of our theological grasp of eschatology, and is treated thoroughly in Chapter 7 of the Constitution on the Church.

Chapter 7 reminds us that "the Church will attain its full perfection only in the glory of heaven, when there will come the time of the restoration of all things." It describes the Church, too, as "the universal sacrament of salvation," and in a spirit of Christian humanism speaks of "the renovation of the world as already anticipated in some real way." [13]

Leading theologians in the Church today stress also the eschatological implications of the sacraments. Karl Rahner, for example, treats Baptism, the Eucharist and the Anointing of the Sick as particularly related to the death of the Christian. In Baptism we die to death in Christ, sharing in the paschal mystery and in Christ's life of grace; our own death subsequently ratifies this, and becomes our confirmation in Christ's grace.

The Eucharist, too, has a special eschatological meaning. It points both to Christ's salvific death, which is in fact the triumph over death, and toward the future glory, of which it is the pledge, which is achieved only after Christ's own triumphant death is shared in. And thus, while the Eucharist is a sacrament of eating, and hence symbolic of life, it is received only as part of the sacrificial banquet. This does not make it less a "celebration," but, rather, a more profound celebration.

The Anointing of the Sick is also a preparation for death, but not in the vastly oversimplified, almost morbid sense that has often been proposed and has entered the Christian imagination. It is precisely a sacrament of healing, and sickness, as we know it after the Fall, is a consequence of sin, a token and prelude to death. In the sacramental anointing we are either restored to health or strengthened to face the final ordeal of death—which itself takes on new meaning as a share in Christ's own death and triumph. In a sense, our most important human act will be our act of dying. It is, in fact, our most personal act. Thanks to Christ in the paschal mystery, we are now able to die redemptively.[14]

In our new appreciation of symbolism, the role of gesture takes on fresh importance and meaning. As long as unintelligible gestures were coupled with unintelligible language, somehow the combination worked. Unintelligibility was in the ecclesiastical air. Various movements did not seem especially confusing, like the position of the priest's hands extended only as far as the shoulder (which, until recently, was actually prescribed), or the missal being transferred back and forth across the altar, the paten hidden under the veil during solemn Masses. One expected bewilderment; it all seemed part of the accepted ceremonial etiquette.

For the priest this etiquette was relatively undemanding, thanks to the use of Latin and the posture which kept his back to the people. Not only could he recite the Latin as fast as he found convenient—since presumably God understands Latin at any speed—but the very tones of the Latin prayers in the sung Mass took care of other possible difficulties. Chanting the Gospel, the priest or deacon could be unperturbed by communication or meaning; his only responsibility was to count to the fourth last syllable of every sentence, where the voice dropped a minor third, and to check ahead for question marks and their special intonation. Further, no one in the congregation was likely to find an error in his counting.

Now, however, in English, the priest must use a manner that will sound priestly, yet not offensively preachy. He cannot utter the word of God or the solemn prayer of the

Church to God in a casual, conversational tone. On the other hand, if he adopts a full dramatic intonation, as though he were playing the role of Hamlet, he will sound affected and "phony," and will thus be anything but effective. Clearly another solution, again not a ready-made one, needs to be worked out.

Shortly before the first Sunday of Advent, 1964, when the vernacular was introduced, the American Bishops' Commission of the Liturgical Apostolate sent out a priests' directive which took this problem into account. Priests were told to practice "careful phrasing and inflection, without exaggerated emphasis or affectation or monotonous patterns of speech." They should see to it that the "message be earnestly communicated in all its meaning." Yet, the directive cautioned, "it is the message that should be remembered, not the one who reads it." Accordingly, the voice should be "reverent without being unctuous, loud without shouting, authoritative without being offensive or overbearing." Further, it should convey sincerity, since this "makes the difference between a matter-of-fact, ritualized, indifferent celebration and one that is truly an expression of faith and devotion." It would not be easy to express better the priest's newly imposed responsibility. Yet every priest who has tried to observe these directives knows how difficult a task is his.

A word should be said about the problem of garb and its symbolic function. It is easy to sympathize with moves toward simplification of clerical vesture and the elimination of all excess in feudal or baroque trappings. For we live in an informal age, where people prefer a garb that suggests less of panoply and more of function than in most centuries of the past. Yet even today, and even at our most relaxed gatherings, we instinctively adopt some element of solemnity. All of us, teen-agers included, feel a compulsion to dress up, with some reference, of course, to the quality of the occasion. While a tuxedo would be grotesque at a picnic, so picnic garb would embarrass even the least formal among us at a cocktail party, graduation or homecoming football game. Some gesture of courtesy, however unstuffy, seems required at any place or event that we deem special. In a sense, some ceremonial dress for special occasions appears to be a constant in human behavior. And not least when one is called to play a special role.

The stern rejection of phoniness today works both ways. Standards and a degree of convention are called for. There is a special symbolism of dress attendant upon initiation ceremonies, whether to fraternities or lodges or even West Side or Liverpool gangs. Granted, of course, the relativity of specific garbs and social conventions. Yet the principle remains that certain manners are prescribed and others anathematized, and it seems a given of human experience.

Accordingly, while the present trend in liturgical garb and liturgical manners is in the direction of forthrightness and simplicity, it is not likely that we shall live to see the abandonment of all ceremony. Our ingrained "need for rites" shows no signs of disappearing—only of being somewhat differently satisfied, more in the direction of what the Constitution calls "noble simplicity."

Happily we have come a long way, at least in those dioceses and parishes where the Church's clear teaching is generously observed, from the following description of the Roman rite as it appeared to an observer only thirty years ago:

"The inner character is often difficult to recognize in its liturgic expression, and especially under the deformations which it so frequently endures through over-familiarity, hurry, indifference or popular misunderstanding. The mut-

tered Low Mass, at which the Ministry of the Word is reduced to the semi-audible recitation of Latin lessons and
the Ministry of the Sacraments to the Communion of the
Priests—the congregation meanwhile pursuing their own
devotions, reciting the rosary, singing hymns, or even listening to a discourse from a loud-speaker." [15]

FOUR

The New Mass

*R*eturning from outer space, or a prolonged sleep, or perhaps from the Diocese of Coma, where the spirit of Vatican Council II has not yet penetrated, what surprises or sources of puzzlement did the Catholic encounter at his first parish Mass during the 1965 transitional period?

In the first place, he discovered that the typical parish church was considerably renovated and modified. Not so many altars or statues, perhaps. The main altar not so removed from the people. In some places, no more communion rail. None of this was likely to mystify him, however, if he had read the chapter on "Liturgy and Fine Arts" later in this book.

Once Mass got started, though, the architectural adjustments began to take on meaning, as the action unfolded. For the priest, instead of standing at the altar with his back to the congregation, was seen to bow solemnly to the altar, engaged in a few preparatory prayers. Meanwhile, the whole congregation sang, or at least recited together, the opening scriptural text called the "entrance hymn" or Introit. It is possible (as he may have heard from his informed neighbor) that a reader, or "commentator," did this instead of the people. In any case, the entrance hymn had become truly an entrance hymn, and this made good sense. The symbol was clear, the Word now understandable.

Following this little ceremony of entrance, which helped to create the mood of the day, the priest moved to his seat in the sanctuary. He faced the people and joined them, singing or reciting, "Lord have mercy"—which made the mysterious words *Kyrie eleison* come to life, in case our observer had ever noticed them before.

"Glory to God in the highest," intoned the priest, as the congregation took up an exciting hymn of praise, every word of which made sense. At this point, facing the people, the priest spread his arms toward them in a meaningful gesture and gave the simplest, most forthright blessing: *Dominus vobiscum!* The only trouble was, our friend had to find his place in the missal to know what the priest was saying— unless, of course, he was in an English-speaking country that used English even here. The people, in Christian courtesy, returned the priest's blessing—stumblingly in Latin, again unless our friend was in another country. Whereupon the priest invited them: *Oremus,* meaning "Let us pray." There followed a few moments of silence, during which everyone could pray quietly, yet somehow together, as a community. Unless, of course, the commentator found it necessary to interrupt the silence to tell the congregation what the priest was about to say in Latin; in many countries, he would not have to interrupt this holy silence, since the priest's prayer, like his invitation to pray, would be in the intelligible vernacular, not Latin.

Then came the Epistle, but with a difference. No longer was it something quietly read out of a missal, as well as one might, trying to catch up with the priest, who was mumbling away toward the altar. Instead, our listener heard a real "proclamation," given as a true message from God, and delivered by the priest or by a deacon or even a fellow layman serving as a minister. But now it made sense. It was directed toward the people. It helped them somehow to feel that they were a community—oh, yes, they used a new expression, "People of God." It made one feel one belonged. And, if someone other than the celebrant read the Epistle, the priest sat down too and listened to God's message. The reading, one noticed, took place from a little pulpit, called ambo, which gave it a special solemnity and seriousness. This must be something important.

Everyone remained sitting after the Epistle, while the choir or reader offered a few moments for recollection and response to God's message. No muttering of half-understood phrases; all serenity in thankful acceptance of the Word of God.

Then another slight ceremony of preparation, symbolizing that something momentous was about to happen. The priest, bowing toward the altar, was obviously praying for God's help. Then he mounted the ambo and read the Gospel as our returned Catholic had never heard it read. It was not rushed through, as though it were something to be disposed of before the serious business of announcements and sermon. Instead, the Gospel itself was a sort of climax. The translation, too, was startlingly new. He remembered that *Gospel* really meant "good news." It was surely a new experience. Even old phrases rang with fresh vigor. And the impact was correspondingly serious too.

And what an unusual sermon, one that really fitted into the Mass as it was unfolding. It seemed not so much a sermon as a sort of overflow of the Gospel—God's own Word coming through in applications to the present. An enriching experience it was, full of Holy Scripture, with stress on the central teachings of the Faith—far removed from the old-time exhortation for more parish funds or Christianity presented in negative terms. God's Word was, after all, exciting. It summoned one to new heights of involvement; it made one want to do something personal for Christ and Christ's people.

The Creed came next. It was not merely listened to or hurriedly followed in the missal. Nor was it a passive experience, listened to as though it were an opera of sorts. The priest started it, but everyone joined in. It no longer seemed the priest's private affirmation of faith, or the choir's opportunity to perform. It belonged to the people. And coming after the Gospel, and that unusual type of sermon, the Creed gave everybody a chance to respond, publicly, socially, with that meaningful new gesture—a bow to Christ as they thanked Him for His blessed coming.

Then the priest's blessing, this time in English: "The Lord be with you!" And a response—"And with your spirit!" —many decibels louder than it had ever been in Latin. Now a new ceremony: a series of prayers that seemed to touch home—not ready-made standard formulas, but prayers for the parish, the country, the world, special needs. Again, not simply five Our Fathers (during which one was expected to forget the words and pray for something else), but prayers that said what they meant, precisely and clearly and without undue repetition. It was easy to join in spirit and aloud.

After these prayers, it was plain that a new point in the Mass had been reached. The priest left the place where he had been standing or sitting, and moved to the altar. This was the first time our participant had ever felt that the altar was an *altar*, and not an elaborate reading stand as well.

While the hosts and wine were brought up—including the

host our visitor had personally placed in the ciborium when he came into church—the people or choir or reader or everybody together shared in scriptural song. This must be what that little snippet called the "Offertory" had been doing in the missal. It really was functional, giving meaning to the priest's preliminary offering as he prepared to enter into the most solemn part of the Mass.

And what a pleasant experience to be able to see what the priest was doing all this time. For now he was facing the people, joined with them yet somehow set a little bit apart with his own special role and function. It all became clear.

The Secret prayer proved to be another surprise. It was no longer "secret." In fact, he might find out that since it had never meant "secret," it was being called "prayer over the oblation." In Latin, *secreta* actually meant the things put aside for the offering, and not, in the liturgy, a "secret" in our ordinary sense. This was a stately, sober prayer—much like the Collect—expressing our offering of ourselves with Christ. Yet, again, to understand this our participant still had to keep one eye on the missal or listen to the commentator; for it was still in Latin, and thus still partly secret.

It ended with *per omnia saecula saeculorum,* to which everyone answered "Amen." It was the ending of the prayer, after all, and not the beginning of the Preface, as it had always seemed. On second thought, he realized that it was strange to have the Preface begin with something so obviously the conclusion of something else.

Then came the people's dialogue with the priest, one of the most venerable parts of the Mass (the notes in his missal told him), but still only half realized, since it was still in Latin. And so was the Preface, which he found in his missal. Suddenly a quick shift of gears and he was in English again: "Holy, holy, holy . . ." Again everyone was involved, sing-

87

ing God's praise in the magnificent words of Old and New Testament, joining in the unnumbered choirs of angels.

Following this outburst came the long prayer of silence, the Canon, which he might follow in his missal or simply join in spirit, in case he found it monotonous to use the same words every day. The priest, still facing the people, renewed the great mystery of Redemption.

If he happened to arrive at church on a day when concelebration (another new word, for which he would have to read our next chapter to understand fully) was taking place, he heard a good deal of the Canon, though still in Latin, and he may have even heard the awesome words of the institution of the Eucharist chanted solemnly. The only time he had ever heard of this was from a friend who had attended a liturgy in one of the Eastern rites. It sounded most impressive now.

Toward the end of the Canon, he noticed another change —a solemn and very moving one. Instead of multiple signs of the cross (which he could never see a reason for, anyway), the priest held up the Host and Chalice, high, so that everyone could see them perfectly. Meantime he recited those stately, mystery-filled words: *Per Ipsum* . . . which our participant was able to understand thanks to his missal. And once again came the phrase *per omnia saecula saeculorum,* to which the congregation, obviously involved, thundered out "Amen!" He might remember having read somewhere that this was the people's great prayer, their ratification of the liturgy, their expression of commitment to Christ in His great sacrificial self-offering. A climactic moment in the Mass, now made almost fully meaningful.

Again back to English, with an invitation to "dare to say Our Father . . ." The Lord's Prayer, shared in by all the

Lord's people, in great stateliness and warmth, said with all possible earnestness, and, of course, said only once, "for keeps." At the end, the priest continued with his arms outstretched, expanding on the last petition—"but deliver us from evil." This prayer, which he had never noticed before, had a technical name, "embolism," but that really didn't matter to him.

He noticed that the priest, while finishing the embolism, broke the Host and put a particle of it into the chalice. An impressive ceremony, yet not completely meaningful. Perhaps some day, as the liturgy continued to be reformed, it would fit in better.

The *Agnus Dei* followed, now understood as an appropriate prayer for mercy and peace, in preparation for Communion. What a simple, understandable, dignified ceremony now surrounded Holy Communion. No hasty signs of the cross with the host as the priest murmured words apparently not meant to be understood. Instead, the celebrant proclaimed simply: "The Body of Christ." And the communicant answered, actively: "Amen," realizing that "Amen" was not to be wistfully translated "so be it," but meant a strong affirmation of Christ and all the consequences of communion with Christ in His offering. Thus, Communion no longer seemed a separate ceremony added on to the Mass, but a sharing in the sacrificial banquet. It occurred to him, too, that after all "communion" does mean sharing, communicating with Christ in His self-giving to the Father.

He felt another change about Communion. It now seemed less private or individualistic, more like a community encounter, with Christ and with the "whole Christ," the people of God. And he found new meaning in the new position, that of standing. Standing, as he received Holy Communion, he felt not less reverent but more involved; the gesture was symbolic of the joy of the paschal mystery, of commitment to Christ, of one's part in the people and work of Christ. Standing suggested activity, especially activity with others. It seemed related to movement, procession and a sense of purpose. And so, for the first time, or at least more clearly than ever before, he realized that Communion and all of liturgy must have a social implication. Further, the fact that everyone was at least trying to sing during the procession up to the altar reminded him of what the Church had often told him before: that Communion unites us with Christ and with all Christ's Mystical Body.

After Communion everything seemed to move swiftly. No Last Gospel. No added prayers. "Go, the Mass is ended," said the priest. The people's reply, "Thanks be to God," sounded just a bit impolite, but not so on second thought. There was a great deal to be thankful for—especially Christ's great self-giving in the Mass. But our participant was also thankful for finding the Mass much more meaningful than ever in the past. True, there remained some rough edges, partly in the unfamiliar things the people had to do, but also (he suspected) partly in the fact that there was still more work to do in the great readjustment and updating of the liturgy that was under way. He felt a few misgivings about the music and, possibly, about some loss of the feeling of devotion as he had formerly known devotion. But he also realized that what he had previously considered a certain amount of mumbo-jumbo, and about which he had once entertained scruples, was now just about gone. He thought that now, with no embarrassment, he could invite his Protestant friends to come to see what a Mass was like. They would find a great deal to understand, and appreciate, and even share in.

We append here a brief sketch of the principal sections of the Mass as they were celebrated before the liturgical reforms and as they are now. Some of the changes that we know took place, at least in some churches, earlier during the liturgical movement. However, the column at the left in our listing that follows does express what was until recently the normal form of celebration in most parishes, while that on the right expresses the present emphasis on participation, distinction of roles, and general clarity and meaningfulness. The priest's position, facing the people, helps identify him with them. He is not performing a solemn spectacle, which they only witness. Rather, together with them—yet with a presidential and consecratory role for which he is ordained— he offers worship to the Father through the Son, the Whole Christ. Yet the people's role is now stressed too. They are not at all, in Pius X's disapproving phrase, "detached and silent spectators," but members of the Whole Christ involved in the work for which they were initiated at Baptism.

	OLD	NEW
Entrance	Priest and servers enter in silence.	During entrance, people sing a processional.
Prayers at foot of altar	Priest and servers.	Priest and servers; these prayers are omitted if a ceremony precedes.
Introit	Priest reads alone.	People say or sing.
Kyrie	Priest and servers.	Priest and people.
Gloria	Priest alone.	People, after intonation by priest.

Collect	Priest alone. Server answers "Amen."	Priest, after pause for people's prayer. People assert their "Amen."
Epistle	Priest alone.	Reader proclaims God's Word.
Gradual and Alleluia	Priest alone.	People speak or sing their response to God's Word.
Gospel	Priest alone.	Priest or deacon.
Homily	Usually none.	Extension of Gospel.
Creed	Priest alone.	People, after intonation by priest.
People's Prayer	None.	People and priest.
Offertory	Priest alone.	People.
Offertory ceremonies	Priest alone.	People bring offerings.
Secret	Priest alone, in silence.	Priest aloud, as people assert their "Amen."
Preface dialogue	Priest and servers.	Priest and people.
Sanctus	Priest alone.	Priest and people.
Canon	Priest alone, in silence.	Priest; sometimes with concelebrating priests, then aloud.
Solemn prayers at end of Canon	Priest alone, in silence.	Priest aloud, and people assert their "Amen."

Pater Noster	Priest alone, in Latin.	People together in vernacular.
Embolism	Priest alone, in silence.	Priest aloud as spokesman for all.
Agnus Dei	Priest alone.	People.
Prayers before Communion	Priest alone.	Priest alone.
Prayers at Communion	Priest alone, in Latin.	Priest and people, in vernacular.
Communion antiphon	Priest alone.	People.
Postcommunion	Priest alone.	Priest, allowing time for people's prayer; and people's "Amen."
Dismissal	Priest and servers.	Priest and people.
Last Gospel	Priest alone.	Omit, since the Mass is over and the Gospel has already been proclaimed.
Added prayers	Priest and people.	Omit, since they are redundant and not very effective.
Various greetings	Priest and servers.	Priest and people.

It seems that nothing could better illustrate how far we have come toward a truly functional liturgy (and the distance we have yet to go) than a close comparison of these two columns. As an elderly lady recently told me: "I thought I was against the changes until I visited a diocese where hardly any of them had taken place. Then I found how much I liked the new way and wondered how I had ever survived under the old dispensation!"

FIVE

Social Meaning
of the Liturgy

The last few years, and most of all those since the opening of Vatican Council II, have been styled variously as "the most troubling" or "the most exciting" since the Reformation era. Much of the choice of epithets, as always, depends on one's age, personality or temperamental predisposition to take bright or dim views. Yet, even after all allowances are made for expected elements of what is probably only good old-fashioned rebelliousness endemic to the human condition, it is not hard to see in today's restlessness an urgent quest for authenticity and against anything that might be taken for sham, phoniness or tokenism.

In part at least, this explains the new freedom of expression that often disturbs or frightens older folk—the agonizing self-criticism and criticism of venerable institutions, the rush to demonstrate or protest, and both the literal and the figurative marches. To the present generation, symbols remain important; indeed they may be more important than ever, so long as they seem genuine. But mere tokens are taboo, whether in the matter of civil rights or within the

Church, in anything that seems to lessen authentic commitment.

Thus, the new breath of the Holy Spirit felt in the Council's two great Constitutions to date—on the Liturgy and on the Church—has been welcomed by men and women who believe themselves very much a part of the present. Such Christians, on reading these great documents, sense a new responsibility, as they become aware of their full-fledgedness, their adult membership in the people of God, their first-class citizenship in the work of the Kingdom.

They sense, too, that worship is now more transparently than ever a social matter—personalist, but not individualistic in orientation, and bearing more than minimal consequences. If the Mass, as they have often heard, is a school of Christianity, its lessons need to be taken out of school and put into daily life. Otherwise they might seem remote, academic, intramural, hence irrelevant to the world Christ loved and gave Himself for. Thus, liturgy has to be something more than a sanctuary enterprise. If one truly participates and shares in the holy work, one has to do the same outside the sanctuary, in the rest of life.

One of our country's foremost liturgists, Father Shawn G. Sheehan, who has long seen and lived the social consequences of liturgy, is very outspoken about the need for making sure that worship flows over into responsible action. "Neither zeal for social action," he cautions, "nor even social consciousness follows automatically from liturgical participation." And he adds a remark that should prove salutary and somewhat humbling: "In fact, it happens more often that persons working together in the social apostolate conceive a desire to worship together." [1]

It may, indeed, be more than a bit humiliating for us Christians to admit that part of the stimulus that prodded us into reaching our new social awareness may have come from even farther from home—in fact, from thinkers and movements that considered themselves very much outside Christianity. One wonders, for example, whether *Rerum Novarum* or *Quadragesimo Anno* (1891 and 1931 respectively), late as they were, would have been written had it not been for the ferment forced on Christendom's attention by Marx, Engels and other professed socialists and Communists of the last century and our own. This is not, of course, to belittle the pioneering, unselfish work of dedicated and saintly Christians during the same periods, much less to imply that the Church's social teaching today is rooted in Marxism.

An elementary example taken from chemical change may illustrate the point. Even the least scientific of us knows that a catalyst is often used to facilitate or speed up a change, without itself entering into the resultant compound. Cultural movements in the past have often affected Christianity, without at the same time changing its inner reality. Feudalism, for example, and other socioeconomic systems are part of Church history as well as secular history. The explosion of geographical and anthropological information in the fifteenth and sixteenth centuries, too, had a great deal to do with the growth of missions and a widening understanding of what was meant by Catholicism.

In a roughly analogous way, too, various modern movements, such as depth psychology and the study of evolution, have served as lenses to sharpen our insights into truths of revelation that we had sometimes left unstressed or less stressed than they are today. To admit that the Church is thus affected by a reality outside its control is really to admit that it is genuinely incarnate in the world, and that it is incarnate in a progressive way. Unflattering as this may

97

seem, it is neither a new nor an unsalutary experience. We should not, then, be altogether shocked if social developments not led by Christians have sometimes served as the goad pushing Christians to self-examination and to deeper realization and fulfillment of parts of their own inheritance.

As we read the record of divine revelation and the divine call to mankind, unless our viewpoint is professedly colored by individualism, we cannot fail to see that both were given largely in social terms. The one prayer Our Lord taught us to say is far from individualistic: God is *Our* Father; we pray for the coming of His *Kingdom;* all our petitions are plural—our plea for forgiveness conditioned by our attitude toward others. Our Lord continually stresses the *general* rather than the particular judgment, and the model criterion for our salvation or rejection is what we do to others. The point needs no expansion.

In *Catholicism,* one of the truly seminal works of twentieth-century Catholic thought, Father Henri de Lubac made this point with special persuasiveness, using phrases that were revolutionary some thirty years ago: "Grace does not set up a purely individual relationship between the soul and God or Christ," he stated; "rather, each one receives grace in the measure in which he is joined socially to that unique organism in which there flows its life-giving stream." [2]

While early Christianity was possessed of a strong social sense, which is constantly preached by the Church Fathers, in the course of time this focus became dulled. Often this was, and still is, not so much the result of positive teaching as of "regrettable omissions" and "the lack of a Catholic mentality," as de Lubac put it. Our problem today, as in any case of reform, is not that of blindly returning to the past, as though the intervening centuries had never existed, but of rethinking in terms of revelation and its impact on the present. In a word, it is what Pope John XXIII meant by a shift of emphasis and a change of heart. "Catholicism," as de Lubac interprets it, "is essentially social. It is social in the deepest sense of the word: not merely in its applications in the field of natural institutions, but first and foremost in itself, in the heart of its mystery, in the essence of its dogma."

The rebirth of scriptural attitudes and awareness has done much to bring this into light. The whole concept of Covenant (*berith*), which is the core teaching of the Old Testament, is not grounded in individualistic piety. God's Covenant is with His *people;* it constitutes them as a people. The holy people is the *Qahal Yahweh* or Assembly of the Lord, gathered by Him to seal the Covenant of Sinai, which Covenant had been anticipated in the Covenant with Noe (Genesis 9:8–17) and that with Abraham (Genesis 17:10–14). This gathered people we find translated by the Septuagint as the *ekklesia,* the precise word used in the New Testament for the new assembly of God's people, or the Church.[3]

We find this theme in both the Constitution on the Liturgy and the Constitution on the Church, but more fully developed in the latter. Pope Paul, in fact, referred to it as "a marvel of fidelity to history, of stupendous sociology, in all of which the divine and the human elements blend to reflect on humanity the outlines of the incarnation and the redemption—the whole Christ Our Saviour." In its opening paragraph, the Constitution sees the Church as "in Christ like a sacrament or a sign and instrument of a very closely knit union with God and of the unity of the whole human race."

Other social descriptions of the Church follow: "a people made one with the unity of the Father, the Son and the Holy Spirit"; the "Kingdom of God inaugurated here on earth"; and a series of "metaphors revealing the nature of the

99

Church." These images are almost entirely social in nature, as we saw above: the family, the building, the temple, the sheepfold, the spouse, the Body of Christ.

Chapter II of that Constitution is titled "On the People of God." It stresses the oneness and interrelation of all: "All the faithful, scattered though they are throughout the world, are in communion with each other in the Holy Spirit." Further, in the Eucharist, "strengthened, they manifest in a concrete way that unity of the people of God which is suitably signified and wondrously brought about by this most holy sacrament." The other sacraments, too, are seen in their social significance; thus, marriage and the family are called "the domestic Church."

In Chapter III, we are reminded that "the human race today is joining more and more into a civic, economic and social unity."

Chapter IV, on the laity, again concentrates on the unity of God's people and the one Body of Christ, as well as on the fact that "all the laity, as a community, must nourish the world with the fruits of the Spirit, diffusing that Spirit which raises up the poor, the meek and the peace-makers." It is especially through the laity that the spirit of Christ will permeate the world, in "justice, charity and peace," so that "the goods of this world may be more equitably distributed among all men and may be conducive to universal progress in human and Christian freedom." Further, in Chapter V, the laity are called to "be of aid to their fellow citizens, raise all of society and even creation itself, to a better mode of existence," thus answering the divine call to holiness.

In this same spirit, the social implications of the liturgy have been pointed out by just about every recent writer on the liturgy or on the social teaching of the Church. One very well-developed treatment is that of the sociologist Father

Michael Campbell-Johnson, in the autumn, 1964, issue of *Thought* magazine. The author relates the biblical, patristic and catechetical movements to the liturgical renewal; then he shows that "many of the results of this theological revival are immediately and obviously social in their application." Not only the Eucharist, where this is most patent, but in all of the sacraments, "whereby the Christian is incorporated into or reconfirmed in the social life of the Mystical Body." [4]

This awareness of how the liturgy, in order to be authentic, must manifest its social implications has been the theme of a growing number of speeches at the annual Liturgical Weeks. It was dramatized most effectively, as I recall, at the Week held at Philadelphia in August, 1963. Just a few days following the Week, the great civil-rights March on Washington was to take place. In a matter of hours, thousands of participants in the Week were seen wearing "March on Washington" buttons, appropriately side by side with their Liturgical Conference badges. And, in fact, hundreds of them did go home to all parts of the country by way of the Washington March.

During the Philadelphia Liturgical Week, speech after speech developed the interracial consequences of the sacramental life, especially of Holy Communion. But the rafters of the great convention hall shook to the applause that repeatedly interrupted Father Godfrey Diekmann's talk on "Sacramental Life—The Mystery Shared." [5] In vigorous, searing phrases, Father Diekmann asserted: "We do not proclaim the death of the Lord; rather, we trumpet the blasphemous triumph of Satan, if we eat of the Bread and drink the cup, and refuse to accept the Negro as our daily table guest!" He went on to draw the general conclusion: "We are guilty of the Body and Blood of the Lord, if we do not share Christ's own love for the body and blood and spirit—if we have no burning concern for equal living conditions and opportunities—of our brother in Christ: Jew or Gentile, colored or white!" Nor was anyone surprised when Father Diekmann appeared to take part in the Selma-Montgomery protest march.

The community-building role of the liturgy is by no means restricted to the sacred banquet, in which all the initiated share in Christ and with each other. For the service of the Word is also social in its dynamism.

In the Old Testament, as Father David M. Stanley has shown, "the Hebrews were created into Israel by Moses' reading of the covenant. And in subsequent eras of history—particularly at critical moments like the religious reform under King Josias or the re-establishment of the exiles in Judaea by the work of Ezra—it was through the recital of God's Word that the people were re-formed, re-constituted and re-united." [6] This is apparent from Chapters 19 and 33 of Exodus, where Moses comes down from Mount Sinai, reads the whole covenant and creates the community. Chapter 5 of Deuteronomy offers a close parallel, and the closing chapter of Joshua is equally relevant to this theme.

Yet this building of the community is not taken as something of the past, as though fossilized. The covenant, after all, is made with living, changeable, existential human beings; it needs repeated renewal. The centrifugal, atomistic tendency of men to go off on their own into egotistic isolation must be constantly corrected. Hence what Father Stanley calls the "up-dating" note in Holy Scripture, in both the Old and New Testaments.

Moses reminds the people of Israel that "the Lord our God made a covenant with us at Horeb; it was not with our forefathers that the Lord made this covenant, but with ourselves, who are all here alive today" (Deuteronomy 5:1–3).

The point is that the source and basis of their life as a community needed to be repeatedly renewed in a liturgical, cultic way.

In the New Testament, too, Christ's covenant in His blood was to be renewed in the Eucharist. Yet this Eucharist is not celebrated alone, apart from the "proclamation": "As often as you eat this bread and drink from this cup," St. Paul says very explicity, "you *proclaim* the death of the Lord until He comes." It is not surprising, then, that the Church uses both the Eucharistic and the Scriptural proclamation in her worship. For, to quote Father Stanley again, "if the Eucharist is Christ's sacramental body, the Scriptures are His sacramental voice." Both these proclamations are made to us as the people of God. Thus both are strongly communitarian and social.

The liturgical action, notably in the Mass, is not that of an undifferentiated mob. There are personal, distinctive roles, and even the people as such keep a measure of difference among themselves. As Maurice Nédoncelle puts it in his phenomenological analysis of prayer, *God's Encounter with Man:* [7] "It might prove quite startling if we could read all that is passing through the mind of each member of the congregation who is praying: what variety there really is behind the apparent uniformity of kneeling forms and hymns in unison!"

While joined as closely as possible in heart and intention in the people of God, all of the persons remain persons. For, as Nédoncelle goes on, "it is not the function of the liturgy to do away with personal freedom, but to enrich its spiritual working. Worship is certainly a discipline, but it is not an extinguisher. It gathers together in one and the same action, Bossuet and Fénelon, a don and a bricklayer, sinners and righteous."

Accordingly, all writers on the liturgy insist on its sense of community. The prayer of the Church, of the people of God, the Body of Christ is "in its very meaning and essence, the prayer of a community; each man enters consciously, if he understands this prayer, into the wider stream of prayer," writes the great lay philosopher Dietrich von Hildebrand in *Liturgy and Personality*.[8] Few prayers apart, the entire liturgy is in terms of "us," not "me." The proportion, the pondus, of liturgical action is social and communitarian.

Further, as von Hildebrand puts it, "liturgical prayer possesses an incomparable communion-forming power." At the same time, as he and other Christian personalist thinkers insist, "in this spirit of communion embodied in the Liturgy, we find one of the most fundamental traits of true personality." For "an isolated man is an unawakened, immature, even a mutilated man." Personalism implies interpersonalism, while individualism or solipsism is closed in on self. While, as recent history demonstrates, mere mass movements lessen men as persons, the liturgical community— based on the encounter with God, and not on mere tribalism —releases us from egocentricity and isolation.

Father Robert O. Johann, a leading American thinker, has put this with great precision, in line with the thought of Teilhard de Chardin: "Not only is God's presence among men the ontological root of their present aspiration toward unity and universal love, but explicit recognition of His presence is a necessary pre-condition for the realization of such love." For the unity of persons as persons arises from the direct relation of each to the one Absolute, a relation that provides the ground of each person's dignity as an individual person, and yet as shared. Thus religion, especially in its social and liturgical dimension, embodies God's presence among us as the ground of our personal union with one another. Thus, "religion is the institutional basis of universal communion." [9]

Plainly, it is most of all in liturgy that religion constitutes this basis. There, above all, the People of God—each person interrelated with every other, with no loss of personal values, and each mutually related with God—finds itself truly one, though not in an impersonal, homogenized way.

As we have suggested, not only the Mass ("Communion" being the ideal form of participation in it) is rich in social symbolism and consequences; all the sacraments, each in its own way, are social phenomena. For in the sacraments the Christian is first initiated, then more and more deeply incorporated, into the Church's life. In them, as Fathers Rahner and Schillebeeckx explain, the Christian encounters Christ and Christ's own activity.[10]

The case may be most apparent in Baptism, the sacrament of initiation *par excellence*. It is, in a special way, the sacrament of Easter, and the Constitution relates it clearly to Easter (Articles 6 and 70).

Confirmation, the Cinderella among sacraments, is also strongly social in character. The Constitution calls for the revision of its rite, in which "the intimate connection which this sacrament has with the whole process of Christian initiation is to be more clearly set forth; for this reason it is fitting for candidates to renew their baptismal promises just before they are confirmed" (Article 71).

Confirmation is, further, the Pentecostal sacrament, in which the Holy Spirit is given us in profusion. It is the sacrament of Christian adulthood and maturity, "inasmuch as it marks the transition from childhood to adulthood. . . . Without confirmation a baptized person is an incomplete Christian in the same way as a child is not yet completely a man." [11]

105

There is still no uniformity of practice regarding the age at which Confirmation should be given. Over the years, the choice has varied widely. Today, the French generally tend to give it early, at about the age of reason, symbolizing that it completes Baptism. A number of other scholars (like Josef A. Jungmann, Canon Drinkwater and Piet Fransen) prefer a somewhat later time, to suggest Confirmation as a sacrament of the apostolate and of personal decision. "It gives the baptized a responsibility for the work of proclaiming Christ as prophets and martyrs," and it "bestows a mission as witnesses." Further, it adds a "further configuration to Christ as Priest," and gives "to our membership and consequently to our worship its social and apostolic dimension." [12]

The term "witness" used often in terms of Christian social commitment, especially with regard to Confirmation, is, in fact, more than a vogue word. It is, rather, a core word of Christianity. In one form or another it occurs hundreds of times in the New Testament. Christ's final command to the Apostles was to be witnesses for Him even to the ends of the earth (Acts 1:8). The Apostles understood this well, and their writings are full of the same charge to become witnesses. Indeed, the early Church is rich in the tradition of the supreme witnessing—which, of course, is the literal meaning of martyrdom.

In this connection, I cannot recommend strongly enough Father Philip Berrigan's chapter, "The Nature of Christian Witness," in *No More Strangers*.[13] Not neglecting the root meaning of being witnesses to Christ, Father Berrigan points to the "heresy" which many Christians today fall into. It is, obviously, a practical not a theoretical heresy, since presumably no serious Christian would subscribe to it in principle. This is the "persistent and paradoxical Christian heresy which takes as the point of departure a witness to God without witness to man, which claims love of God, but fears love of man, which in reality is a selfish and pragmatic ethic." Father Berrigan further describes it as "a philosophy that will pad and cushion one from the demands of life, or allow us to deal with only its more palatable forms, justifying a contact with life that is peculiarly detached and contemptuous."

The remedy to this practical heresy is found, of course, in the much lauded but equally much neglected encyclicals of Pope John, *Mater et Magistra* and *Pacem in Terris,* and in the many pronouncements of the Council on Christian responsibility. From the liturgy, as we understand it today, "the Christian must absorb the testimony and dynamism of Christ—he must accept His commission, and embark with Christ on a work of healing and reclamation." Father Berrigan quotes Pope Paul, too: "It is necessary to remake Christian society; it is necessary to awaken it, to be aware that we are responsible. We are responsible for our times, for the life of our brothers and we are responsible before our Christian conscience." The whole of Father Berrigan's challenging book is a blueprint for the Christian who is willing to be an authentic Christian, who is willing to take up the social and human gauntlet given him in Baptism and Confirmation, and again in the other sacraments.[14]

The sacrament of Penance, too, has its social dimension. True, with the strong preoccupation with privacy and secrecy with which confession has been hedged in for some centuries, Penance has come to be thought of as above all a private sacrament. Further, the strict tradition of "the seal of confession" is so much a part of the Catholic ethos, with its elaborate canonical defenses, that it is hard to imagine Penance in social terms.

107

Yet, the sin of the Christian is not only a private matter. It is also a sin against the Christian community, as Father Rahner has stressed.[15] This is especially evident in the case of notorious scandal. But even lesser sins are in some sense public, at least as a failure in the Christian to witness to the holiness that has come into the world in Christ. Accordingly, the early Church made a great deal of public penance, and liturgical theologians today are trying to work out ways of restoring this ancient practice in a form that fits today's needs. This would not, of course, imply any change in the privacy or secrecy of confession, but might possibly take the form of public absolution after several private confessions.

Excommunication has become such a rarely invoked penalty in our time that we may tend to overlook the "binding" power of the Church, which is a correlative to her "loosing" power. Even so, the obligation to receive the sacrament of Penance at least on certain occasions is minimally social: one must present oneself to the Church, as personified in the visible presence of the priest who absolves from excommunication. The fact, too, that Penance is normally administered in a church, where everyone may at least see the penitent enter the confessional, is some residue of its social symbolism and character.

Matrimony and Holy Orders are even more evidently social in their meaning and consequences. The Constitution on the Liturgy calls for the marriage ceremony to be "revised and enriched in such a way that the grace of the sacrament is more clearly signified" (Article 77), and the fact that it is now "normally to be celebrated within the Mass, just before the Prayer of the Faithful" (Article 78), further symbolizes its ecclesiastical and communitarian meaning. "Both the ceremonies and texts of the ordination rites are to be revised" (Article 76), and permission is given for some use of the vernacular, which will obviously enable the faithful to participate more meaningfully and socially.

Finally, the sacrament of Extreme Unction has been happily renamed the Anointing of the Sick. The Constitution (Article 73) goes out of its way to assure us that it "is not a sacrament reserved for those only who are at the point of death." It is, rather, for those who begin "to be in danger of death from sickness or old age." This surely makes it possible for the Anointing to be a social event, more of a family sacrament, at which relatives and friends may be present to lend their prayerful support and join in the sacramental act of the whole Church.

There are two crucial texts in the Acts of the Apostles which say a great deal about the nature of the primitive Church just after the coming of the Holy Spirit. "They continued steadfast in the apostles' teaching and in fellowship, in the breaking of bread and prayers" (Acts 2:42–43). The other: "They that believed were of one heart and soul and . . . had all things in common" (Acts 4:32).

It is more than coincidental that the word for "common" —*koina*—and that for "fellowship"—*koinonia*—are very nearly the same word. Until the liturgical renewal began, it seems that we seldom heard these texts discussed, unless it was to make clear that the second concerned something restricted to the early Church and was not meant as an endorsement of communism or an attack on the sacredness of private property. And the very term "fellowship," too, sounded vaguely Protestant and was hardly popular in stanchly Catholic circles. (Though Monsignor Ronald Knox does use "fellowship," in his translation of the Bible.)

One of the very moving writers of our century, Dietrich Bonhoeffer (the young German theologian murdered by the Nazis in 1945), brings out the relevance of these texts: "Fellowship is mentioned between Word and Sacrament; this is no accident, for fellowship always springs from the Word and finds its goal and completion in the Lord's Supper." He shows, further, that "the whole common life of the Christian fellowship oscillates between Word and Sacrament; it begins and ends in worship." [16] This is a penetrating insight into the social implications of the liturgy.

How our commitment is to take place in detail is, as Father Rahner has repeatedly pointed out, no matter of a predetermined formula or recipe. True, "it is only when a Christian is aware of the commandment to love his neighbor, and through that of his responsibility for the world, that he is really a Christian." [17] Nevertheless, this is only the beginning; and "we have got to have the courage to act as human beings with a task in the world of history." [18] The Church does have a body of social teaching, but, apart from given specific situations, it is not spelled out in such detail as to free us from our need to do a great deal of technical work. Otherwise, our Christian commitment will be thoroughly ineffectual, and far from the true justice and love which are our vocation. As has been well observed, Christ came to save us, but He did not come to save us from trouble.[19]

Yet, far as most of us are from achieving a full Christian response, as a group I believe we have progressed some distance from the days when G. K. Chesterton could quip:

> The Christian Social Union was very much annoyed.
> For there are social evils which we really should avoid.
> And so they sang a lot of hymns—to help the unemployed.[20]

SIX

Liturgy and Ecumenism

$\mathcal{C}$atholic worship is becoming more Protestant and Protestant worship more Catholic." This epigram is no "traditionalist" charge, or the eager *bon mot* of some iconoclast, but is one of the last recorded sentences of a scholar who may have done as much as anyone in this country to base the liturgical movement on serious dogmatic and historical principles. Father Gerald Ellard made this statement at the 1963 Harvard Roman Catholic-Protestant Colloquium just a few days before he received the last sacraments.

Despite the fact that a noted authority made this statement, some will find it disquieting, just as others will believe it overly optimistic. For the ecumenical trends of our time may be said to be still in their infancy. Further, the liturgical developments taking place in the Catholic Church and in most Protestant churches can hardly produce the instant ecumenism hoped for by enthusiasts. Four hundred years of polemics, and the abysmal divergences in spiritual and cultural tradition between Catholics and Protestants, cannot be swiftly bridged even by far-reaching liturgical reforms.[1]

Yet we should not be too cynical to observe signs of hope.

111

They were expressed with considerable wit by Dr. Robert McAfee Brown, the eminent Presbyterian theologian and observer at Vatican Council II, whose volume on the Council is one of the most charitable and balanced yet to appear: "For a long time we hated one another. Then we ignored one another. Then we began talking to one another. Then we began praying for one another. And now we are beginning to pray with one another. And when that is a fact, no one can safely erect barriers around where the relationship may go from here." [2]

In recent years it has become common enough for a person to enter a church building constructed in contemporary style and to spend some minutes unsure whether it is Catholic or Protestant. Anyone can match my own experience of going into a new church in the Midwest, and only after a few minutes asking my guides: "What denomination?" I was not entirely surprised to be told: "Baptist." It would have been even less surprising had they said Episcopal or Lutheran or Methodist. In the past few years, too, illustrated volumes have appeared on contemporary church building, in which one has to read the notes to be sure whether an individual structure is Catholic or not. [3]

It is not merely, or even mainly, that the newer Catholic churches are simplified and stripped of ornament, in such a way as to resemble churches in the Reformed tradition. When we read an architectural directive that images and their number "should be moderate . . . otherwise they may create confusion among the Christian people and foster devotion of doubtful orthodoxy," and that "liturgical architecture provides the space and tools in which the central acts of the Christian life are performed in the common worship of God," no longer are we surprised to learn that the first quotation is from Vatican Council II's Constitution on the Sacred Liturgy (Article 125), while the second comes from a Methodist theologian, Dr. James F. White.[4] In fact, Dr. White devotes a good deal of space to discussing matters like the relative position of altar and lectern, and other topics of concern to Catholics too.

Only a few years ago it was a rather general impression that the liturgy would be one of the very last hurdles to be encountered by ecumenists. We Catholics had long been accustomed to criticism of certain Catholic practices— "prayer wheels, worship of the dead, affirmation of rites with forgotten meanings," to use the caricature presented in a chorus of T. S. Eliot's *The Rock.* For years, too, with varying gestures of patience or condescension, we had repeatedly tried to explain our liturgical ceremonies, both to our own people and to friendly outsiders. Even so, it was hard to dissipate uneasiness, even among Catholics, about what often looked like magic, or at best a needless overgrowth of secondary practices at the expense of the primary. The late Pope John XXIII had found it advisable, during his reign, to caution priests against certain "excessive devotions" that sometimes made "the whole picture tarnished and impoverished." [5]

As a leading Catholic historian of the Reformation, Joseph Lortz, has pointed out, much of the cause of what happened in the sixteenth century lay in a "questionable and fragmentary kind of Catholicism, evidenced by a frantic externalization of popular religious practices." Even more, he shows, there was widespread deterioration in the liturgy itself, shown in the "downgrading of the main altar and the community Mass, the bond of unity." [6] I believe it could be demonstrated, were there space here, that the unintelligibility, and hence the relative dysfunctionality, of the medieval liturgy, contributed to the lack of balance between "of-

113

ficial" and "popular" devotion, which the Reformers found so objectionable.

As we know, the Council of Trent (1545) set out earnestly to reform the more evident and rampant abuses. For one thing, it ordered "frequent explanations during Mass of what is being read and explanations of the mystery of the Holy Sacrifice." [7] However, this and other constructive prescriptions of Trent went all but unobserved for a number of centuries. Further, some of the reforms called for by the Council were based on rudimentary historical and patristic research, and while they were surely far superior to what they set out to replace, they left much to be desired by modern standards of liturgiology. Accordingly, there followed what has been called "the epoch of changelessness or rubricism" [8]—stress on ceremonial detail.

In the inevitable climate of controversy that immediately followed the Reformation, it is not surprising that the stress in liturgy, as in some other areas of Catholic teaching, was repeatedly placed on those points where Catholics and Protestants differed most widely. Where the Reformers were most concerned about the primacy of the Word, Catholics insisted on keeping the Word in Latin, a language understood by only the educated elite. Instead of homilies based on the scriptural passages read in Latin at Mass, preachers were inclined to weave elaborate apologetic or speculative sermons which often achieved peaks of oratory and erudition, but usually accentuated specifically "Catholic" positions, rather than the Christian teachings that we held in common. Love of the Bible even came to be thought of as a trait of Protestantism.

To the Protestants, emphasis on the priesthood of all the faithful, Catholic practice opposed a ritual ever more clerical in appearance, and indeed in inspiration. Where

Protestants tended to see the sacraments only as signs of faith, Catholics stressed the *ex opere operato* principle—putting the emphasis on the causality of the sacraments themselves, rather than on our personal responsiveness. And some uninstructed Catholics stressed it in a way that bordered on magic, when it did not cross the border.[9] Father Louis Bouyer, who is deeply read in Protestant theology, has called to our attention Luther's famous attack on Catholic treatments of the sacraments in his *De Captivitate Babylonica*. In Luther's eyes, the Church of his day projected the image of an enormous pumping machine supposed to enable us to draw upon the merits of Christ and the saints; to this end, it terminated in several large taps, while near each of these taps stands a priest ready to turn it on and make it give a few drops every time someone comes and pays the right fee.[10]

Despite certain efforts, which would have to be mentioned if this were a historical survey, the divisions between Christians widened with time. During the nineteenth century, before our modern liturgical renewal got well under way, the cleavage between Catholic and Protestant worship had become wider than ever, reflecting the tragic fact that Catholics and Protestants were "farther away in sympathy than ever."[11]

Meantime, a curious paradox had arisen with regard to the liturgy and ecumenism. One of the central positions of Protestantism is, of course, the emphasis on the individual's personal encounter with God; thus, less stress is placed on the ecclesiastical function. Catholicism, on the other hand, stresses the Church as the sacrament of Christ, and, accordingly, the need for membership in the Church. Yet, precisely because the Catholic liturgy was relatively unintelligible, thanks in part to the use of a hieratic language not grasped by most of the laity, Catholics leaned more and more toward solitary, individualistic prayer and private devotions. Protestants, meanwhile, worshiping in the vernacular, were able to develop a much stronger sense of participation and community in their social worship. Thus, the two systems had in fact crossed, liturgically, without ever meeting, indeed without even approaching each other. This paradoxical situation is one of the sad ironies of the divisions of Christendom.

It is a happy fact, and not a surprising one, that the Council's Constitutions on the Sacred Liturgy and on the Church, with their strong scriptural flavor, are already doing a great deal to allay Protestant suspicions that Catholics really are unconcerned about the Word of God. There is little indeed, in the key fifth and sixth articles of the Constitution on the Liturgy, at which a Protestant would balk or feel uncomfortable. Further, many Protestants would find it easy to accept the succeeding six articles, so positive is their emphasis on Holy Scripture. And no Protestant, I suppose, would be unmoved by the sentence in Article 7 that states: "[Christ] is present in His Word, since it is He Himself who speaks when the holy scriptures are read in the Church." On the other hand, many a "traditionalist" Catholic might be uneasy.

The whole tenor of the Constitution on the Sacred Liturgy may be described as ecumenical. The very first article, for example, specifies among the reasons for undertaking the reform of the liturgy the desire "to foster whatever can promote union among all who believe in Christ." Article 14 alludes to the priesthood of the laity and cites relevant texts from St. Peter's first epistle (2:9 and 2:4–5), about the Christian people as a "chosen race, a royal priesthood, a holy nation, a redeemed people." The immediate consequence is seen as the "full, conscious, and active participation in liturgical celebrations which is demanded by the very nature of the liturgy."

Further, this participation by the laity is "their right and duty by reason of their Baptism." Pius XII, in his *Mediator Dei* (Paragraph 92), had already spoken of the laity's "share in the priesthood of Christ Himself," grounded on their Baptism and membership in Christ the Priest. Yet the new Constitution goes ever further. Serious liturgical participation is repeatedly insisted on throughout: "In the restoration and promotion of the sacred liturgy, this full and active participation by all the people is the aim to be considered before all else" (Article 14). Pastors are ordered to promote "with zeal and patience . . . the liturgical instruction of the faithful, and also their active participation in the liturgy both internally and externally" (Article 19; cf. also Articles 11 and 56). Last Christmas, as I was celebrating Mass, a zealous priest who was acting as commentator exhorted the faithful in these words: "You've been singing like angels. Now I'm going to ask you to do even better: sing like Baptists!" An ecumenical gesture, if ever there was one.

Little wonder that in a sympathetic article written for *Christianity and Crisis* (January 6, 1964), Dr. Robert McAfee Brown praised the Constitution on the Sacred Liturgy as "the Council's most substantial achievement to date, and possibly one that will stand as the most solid achievement of the entire Council." This was written, of course, before the great Constitution on the Church and the Decree on Ecumenism, which, I suppose, Dr. Brown would want to include together with the liturgical document. In any case, they are in the same ecumenical direction.

Among the points which he finds most basic and revolutionary are: the wide use of the vernacular in all the sacra-

117

ments (this, in fact, surprised even the most sanguine of us, who hardly expected the *form,* or core words, of the sacraments to be allowed in the vernacular); the extensive use of the vernacular in the Mass; the greater liturgical participation by the laity; the greater stress on Holy Scripture and the homily. But most of all, he states, and I see no reason to disagree, the Council's "intent throughout is to insure that worship is *the act of the people* and not simply a spectacle performed for them by the priest."

Two other important developments in Catholic liturgy made by the Constitution are mentioned by Dr. Brown, and we may say a word about them now: concelebration (the celebration of one Mass by more than one priest at a time), and Communion under both kinds (bread and wine). Both of these, under frequent and animated discussion among liturgists, were seldom thought of by the average Catholic. Had he been asked about them, he might even have answered (once he had found out what the words mean) that concelebration was all right for ordination ceremonies but made no sense otherwise, and Communion under both kinds was simply Protestant or, at best, acceptable for the Eastern rites.

In the past year, however, concelebration has sprung suddenly into the visual imagination of Catholics, thanks largely to pictures or newscasts of ceremonies in St. Peter's basilica. One was the opening ceremony of the Council's third session, when the Pope concelebrated the Mass with a group of Council Fathers from all parts of the world. Another was the concelebration that took place on January 25, when new cardinals offered Mass, again at the high altar, together with the Holy Father. Finally, during Holy Week of 1965, many Catholics had a chance to witness concelebration in their own churches.

Yet interest among scholars was by no means new.[12] True, most theologians from the Middle Ages to the beginnings of the liturgical movement showed little interest in the subject, and Canon Law simply forbade it except at ordinations of priests and consecrations of bishops, where it took a peculiar form, which most liturgists find rather unsatisfactory for several reasons. For one thing, the newly ordained were not allowed to receive from the consecrated chalice. Further, the recitation, together with the Bishop, of all the prayers of the Canon showed no distribution of roles, but only, as Jungmann suggests, the idea of putting the Holy Order just received "to practical proof."

Interest, however, arose in great part through the gradual growth of study and sympathy for Eastern liturgies (where concelebration is a rather normal thing), and through the mounting realization of the social and communal character of the Mass stimulated by concelebration. At gatherings of liturgists and priests, the topic increasingly came up for discussion, especially since at such gatherings it seemed a great loss for each priest to go off to a private (sometimes roughly improvised) altar for his own individual celebration. In the course of time, theologians of the stature of Karl Rahner began probing the question, in terms of speculative theology, in articles that proved quite controversial and enlightening back in the early 1950s.

Thus, the words of the Constitution came as a sort of bombshell to people who had not kept up on theological or liturgical literature. For concelebration was not only allowed, but positively praised. Article 57 of the Constitution on the Liturgy starts: "Concelebration, whereby the unity of the priesthood is appropriately manifested, has remained in use to this day in the Church both in the east and in the west. For this reason it has seemed good to the Council to

119

extend permission for concelebration to the following cases . . ." The cases refer to Masses on Holy Thursday and those during Councils and Bishops' meetings, and at the blessing of an abbot; in addition, the bishop may give permission for concelebration on other occasions when it is judged opportune. Article 58 called for a new rite for concelebration to be drawn up. This new rite, which appeared on March 27, 1965, took advantage of forms developed in places where concelebration was practiced experimentally over a period of more than a year.

We know now that concelebration was a common practice in the early Church, but our liturgical documentation of the period is too sparse for us to know what the ceremonies were like. The theologian Mother Jean C. McCowan has studied all available material on the subject and presented her findings in a useful volume, *Concelebration,* and in an article, "Modes of Concelebration and Their Relative Value." [13]

The key concept is, of course, that expressed in the Constitution: "whereby the unity of the priesthood is appropriately manifested." Its ecumenical and symbolic import lies partly in the gesture toward Churches of the East, and partly on the stress on the priesthood as really one in Christ, the supreme Priest.

Perhaps even more significant in ecumenical terms is the new attitude expressed toward Communion under both kinds. It is treated in Article 55, where it is strongly recommended that the faithful receive Communion "from the same sacrifice"—indeed, it is called "that more perfect form of participation in the Mass." Then, after confirming the dogmatic principles about Communion which were laid down by the Council of Trent (Session 21, held July 16, 1562, defends Communion under one kind as a valid and even a useful development in the Church's experience), the Constitution goes on: "Communion under both kinds may be granted when the bishops think fit, not only to clerics and religious, but also to the laity." The permission is thus not unrestricted, but has been rather widely extended by a recent decree of the Holy See (March 7, 1965). A number of cases are explicitly allowed as of now: for the newly ordained priest at the Mass of ordination (the previous custom of having the new priest drink from a chalice of unconsecrated wine was certainly bizarre); to religious at the Mass of their profession and at their jubilees; to newlyweds at their nuptial Mass; to newly baptized adults, and several similar cases.

While, unlike the case of concelebration, the reason for the new practice of Communion under both kinds is not made explicit, as Father Godfrey Diekmann has put it, it was "obviously concern for fullness of sign." [14] And Father Adrien Nocent, writing before the Constitution was promulgated, had urged its restoration, on the grounds that "younger generations of Christians are responsive to it, and not because they are attracted by a novelty, but because they are more aware of the value of the sign." [15] For the *full* sign of the Eucharistic banquet includes both the eating and the drinking, not just one or the other.

In our Roman rite, customs with respect to Communion have varied notably in the course of history. Until the Middle Ages, it was customary to receive the Host from the priest and the cup from the deacon. The priest or deacon said: "The Body of Christ" or "The Blood of Christ," and the recipient answered: "Amen." We have seen at least the first part of this ceremony restored recently. The Eastern rites have kept Communion under both kinds, but with a number of variations in detail. In the West, however, the custom of giving the chalice to the laity was generally dropped sometime in the Middle Ages, perhaps for reasons of cleanliness or danger of profanation.[16] Regrettably, at the time of the Reformation the issue became so heated that, somewhat like the vernacular case, Communion under one species gradually came to seem to Catholics a matter of orthodoxy or heresy. Today, in our more ecumenical climate, it is again possible to discuss the subject serenely, and to accept the values—symbolic and very real—of the fuller, more expressive sign. For Our Lord did say "all of you drink of this," and the participation under both species is surely a more meaningful sign of the Eucharistic banquet. It may be hoped that permission for its wider use will be extended to groups that are small enough to make the richer ceremony feasible.

Further, anyone who has participated in the rite in one of the Eastern liturgies knows that it involves no real danger or appreciably greater length of time. And I have yet to meet anyone who has actually received Communion under both kinds and failed to find it a rewarding experience—and this quite apart from the novelty or "shock" value.

The Constitution contains nothing explicit about another development in the practice of Communion: that of receiving while standing. Again, with few dissenters, I have found that people commonly find this expressive and helpful once they actually experience it. It is the more ancient custom and seems more perfectly to symbolize our joy in participating in the paschal banquet, since kneeling is rather a symbol of penance than of joy. Taken alone, this may have little ecumenical importance. Yet the overtones of this gesture are helpful: they mark a return to a practice that goes back to a period before the divisions of Christendom—in this case the division between Orthodox and Catholics, which is even older than that between Protestants and Catholics. For another reason, the symbolism of standing at Communion is somewhat less "clerical" in appearance. Too, its suggestion of the banquet element in the Eucharist is closer both to the Orthodox and to certain Anglican and Lutheran traditions than is the rather one-sided post-Tridentine focus on adoration of the Blessed Sacrament, rather than the more sacramental "use" of the Blessed Sacrament.

Not long ago the Protestant historian Karl August Meissinger affirmed: "If Luther were to return today he would be amazed to find a Roman Church which he would never have attacked, as it is seen today." This may be an overstatement, but it strongly points to the fact that many of the features of Catholic practice, as Luther knew them, have been rectified, especially those connected with the liturgy.

But even more ecumenically relevant than any single change in the liturgical Constitution is the entire spirit of the document. Here the Church sees herself—as indeed is made more explicit in the Constitution on the Church—as a people, the people of God, using a most scriptural and traditional image. While authority is expressed, there are none of the undertones of that type of authoritarianism that has so alienated non-Catholics. Also, the stress on Christ as our Mediator, indeed (in Article 60 of the Constitution on the Church) on Christ as our sole Mediator in the strict biblical sense, will surely help alleviate anxieties on the part of those who misunderstood Catholic devotion to Mary and the saints.

I had the privilege of being present at some of the sessions of Vatican Council II. It was touching to watch the Orthodox and Protestant observers during the celebration of the liturgy, and their varying ways of expressing reverence. Some stood austerely at strict attention, others bowed profoundly, others knelt, others made many signs of the cross as in Eastern rites. Despite the differences, all seemed united in intention and heart. This repeated experience of the Council may, in the perspective of history, prove one of the most authentically momentous and germinal. The variety was moving; yet there was poignance, too, as one realized that we have not yet achieved the degree of union desired by Christ.

The Council's later Decree on Ecumenism (November 21, 1964) makes a number of points that bear directly on the liturgy. Article 5, for example, points with happiness to the fact that "the brethren divided from us also use many liturgical actions" in common with us, and that "these liturgical actions must be regarded as capable of giving access to the community of salvation." Then, in words that would be acceptable to orthodox Protestant theologians, the Decree insists that "all who have been justified by faith in baptism are members of Christ's body, and have a right to be called Christian, and so are with solid reasons accepted as brothers by the children of the Catholic Church."

Somewhat later, in Article 7, the Decree points with ecumenical hope to the present work of Church renewal in several spheres. Among those explicitly mentioned are "the biblical and liturgical movements, the preaching of the Word of God and catechetics and the apostolate of the laity"—the very themes which we are attempting to explore in this book. The Decree sees in them "promises and guarantees for the future progress of ecumenism."

Regarding the Churches of the East, the Decree mentions "the great love with which they celebrate the sacred liturgy, especially the eucharistic mystery, source of the Church's life and pledge of future glory." Indeed, "through the celebration of the Holy Eucharist in each of these Churches, the Church of God is built up and grows in stature, and through concelebration their communion with one another is made manifest." This section from Article 16 surely opens up astonishing vistas of ecumenism that would have been altogether unthinkable just a few years ago.

With regard to the "separated Churches of the West," the Decree finds bonds of liturgical unity too: "Baptism establishes a sacramental bond of unity which links all who have been reborn by it." And, while the Decree does not accept the sacramental orders of Protestant Churches, and hence not "the proper reality of the eucharistic mystery in its fullness," it gladly recognizes that "when they commemorate His death and resurrection in the Lord's Supper, they profess that it signifies life in communion with Christ and look forward to His coming in glory" (Article 23). This last may be the most amazingly ecumenical statement of the whole Decree.

At the Harvard Roman Catholic-Protestant Colloquium mentioned at the beginning of this chapter, the distinguished Protestant professor of Union Theological Seminary, Dr. Cyril C. Richardson, made this important observation: "It is likely that the Catholic services will become more like Protestant ones just as, under the impetus of the current liturgical revival, Protestant services are recovering something of their Catholic past and becoming more like Roman ones." He concluded: "This presages well for an eventual unity of the spirit among Christians in so far as they appreciate the many diverse facets of worship and grow closer together in their common concern for the life of Christ." [17]

And while no one expects the liturgical renewal to be the sole instrument of healing for what Pope Paul has called "the burden of history," it would be wanting in Christian hope not to accept the present liturgical movements, in both Catholic and other churches, as providential in our time.[18]

125

It should be evident, too, that a deeper grasp of the liturgy, and its great themes of salvation history and the Old Testament, will go far toward increasing awareness of our debt to Judaism and our links with this noble religious tradition. The point seems too obvious to require expansion here.[19]

Finally, I must recommend a recent and most sympathetic volume, *Sacraments and Orthodoxy*, by Father Alexander Schmemann, a leading Orthodox theologian and dean of St. Vladimir Seminary. Father Schmemann dedicates his work to the pioneers and developers of the Catholic liturgical renewal, mentioning several of them by name (Odo Casel, Lambert Beauduin, J. A. Jungmann, Louis Bouyer, Romano Guardini and H. A. Reinhold). He then states, with great ecumenical sympathy: "It is not an exaggeration to affirm that it was precisely the liturgical movement which, even before the organized ecumenical movement began, was the first to break through the ignorance and indifference, to create the possibility of a new encounter, no longer in fear and suspicion, but in love and mutual respect and, above all, on a common ground." [20]

SEVEN

Liturgy and the Arts

Of all truisms uttered about the fine arts, it may be that the only one that stands up under scrutiny is their radical connection with religion, and in the broad sense, with liturgy. Even the paleolithic paintings on the cave walls of Lascaux and Altamira, for all their naturalness, suggest at least a clearly magical, if not precisely religious, tonality. All of us who have spent some time in these caves have felt this unmistakably, and professional anthropologists corroborate our spontaneous impressions. Ethnomusicologists, too, insist on the sacral impulse at the origins of much, if not all, music. Musicologist Siegfried Nadel goes so far as to theorize that music began as an instrument of communication between man and the supernatural, and E. O. James, the distinguished archeologist, in the very title of his most recent work, *From Cave to Cathedral,* implies the same general theme. For, with few exceptions, the supreme artistic expressions, as well as the earliest, have dealt with the numinous, the divine, the liturgical.

All this is cheery enough to the Christian involved in the fine arts. The recent epoch of art and music, however, emerges

127

as a troubling exception. While the reasons for this are doubtless complex and elusive, in part they must have to do with the lack of vigor shown by Christianity in the nineteenth century, which, as Christopher Dawson recently said, "was a new century and a new world in which the Church was almost a stranger." [1] Further, the separation between the artist and the Church has led to a vacuum in which each has been the loser.

When the Constitution on the Liturgy asserts that "Holy Mother Church has . . . always been the friend of the fine arts and has ever sought their noble help" (Article 122), the reader grounded in art history feels that the Council Fathers must have been bravely keeping a stiff upper lip. For the immediate past of sacred art has been, in very large part, a wasteland.

Accordingly, Pope Paul's voice is said to have quivered and his eyes filled with tears when he spoke at the Mass of the Artists, at St. Peter's on Ascension Thursday, 1964. He pleaded earnestly for a "new pact of reconciliation" between religion and the arts after the tragic divorce just mentioned. In a gesture of admirable humility he granted that much of the blame lay on churchmen who have "imposed imitation upon you as a primary canon, upon you who are creators." He then added, "We have insisted on this or that style or tradition to be followed; we have set up these canons from which you must not deviate; we have oppressed you at times as it were with a cloak of lead." He then offered his generous *mea culpa:* "For this we beg your pardon."

It was Chapter VII of the Constitution that the Holy Father pointed to as the "new alliance" between the Church and artists. And, indeed, well he might. For, while in recent years a great proportion of the Church's legislation on art and sacred music had been largely cautionary, if not altogether restrictive, this chapter (and Chapter VI, on sacred music) is altogether positive, even optimistic in tone. There appears scarcely a single "don't."

Paradoxically, this new mood of receptiveness and openness shining through the Constitution also raises problems. On the one hand, it is difficult to persuade artists that we mean what we say—that they and their work are truly welcome—that we really believe that "very rightly the fine arts are considered to rank among the noblest activities of man's genius" (Article 122), and that artists "are engaged in a kind of sacred imitation of God the Creator" (Article 127). On the other hand, religious people have been nurtured on the most reactionary, repetitive, cliché-ridden products of religious art, not to mention the mood of suspiciousness against anything that smacks of "modern art," by which they have been surrounded since infancy. Of more than one massive ecclesiastical building in the recent past could it be said that this was "the devil's revenge"—so fully had churchmen seemed to turn their backs on whatever was vital or fresh in architecture and art.

A gloomy commentary, done doubtless with the most laudable intentions and hence the more piteous, on the overwhelming bulk of recent sacred art, appeared in the General Motors exhibit at the recent New York World's Fair. As you whirred through the exhibit's vision of the future along the Futurama ride, you beheld the face of our cities transformed "in new beauty and strength" (as the electronic guide cheerfully assured you). Dwarfed by buildings of immense scope, some of them done with strikingly imaginative design, you saw pitiful little neo-Gothic churches, while the guide, in appropriately reverent tones, comforted you with the promise that "traditions and faiths would be preserved." This seemed to suggest that, amid the important business of real life, religion and its symbols would remain unchanged, ever irrelevant, like cozy oases where one might escape into some pleasant past.

Even so, architecture is in a comparatively privileged position as compared to the other fine arts. After all, while even the least competent novice suffers from no scruples when composing a new hymn or daubing a picture of the Sacred Heart, everyone knows that a building has to stand up. However conventional and unimaginative, not to say antifunctional, a church might be, it will almost invariably be put up by a contractor with at least a minimum amount of skill; for if the building tumbles down during construction, or shortly thereafter, no fee will be forthcoming.

Not so with the less palpably dangerous arts: a Mass or motet may come apart, but no one is physically crushed by the débacle. Nor is the havoc of a saccharine painting immediately evident. On the other hand, a bad building has a way of being disastrously lasting, and the financial investment that went into it makes its dismantling most unlikely, regardless of the damage done to the parish liturgical life, not to mention its aesthetic life.

A church is a building, and as such must create an environment. This must be a special kind of environment, called for by certain specific events that are to take place in the given building. Indeed, one may say that it must be a sort of "anti-environment." It cannot be unrelated to our normal environment, however; else it will prove merely escapist, or cuddly, or otherwise impertinent. At the same time, a church is a building with a difference. It is directed toward the use of the people of God, whom it must serve and express.

Further, it serves and expresses the people of God not simply as they are gathered, but as they are gathered with a purpose, as a community. As the great theologian Father Bernard Cooke put it, the church must "open on to the mystery of the presence of Christ as sent from the Father and as working in the community." Thus it must do at least two things: help in the communication of the Word and in the people's response to the Word; and suggest, clearly and cogently, the basic banquet-sacrifice structure of the principal liturgical act. Its other functions are secondary, and what happens on Sunday, when the whole community is present, is immeasurably more determining than what happens the rest of the week.

The church building's "holiness" must be expressed in incarnational (God-man) and redemptional (paschal) terms. It thus differs profoundly from a pagan temple, and even from the temple of Jerusalem, which were seen as dwelling places of the divinity. It creates a dynamic rather than a solely contemplative space. It is, of course, a "house of God," but mainly in the sense of a "house of God's people." After all, God needs no temple or house built with hands; it is His people that need the holy place.[2]

It goes without saying that this present chapter does not presume to instruct architects or other artists in how to achieve a liturgical purpose. Anyone, be he priest or hired builder, will naturally go to the specialized literature on the subject (some of which is in our Suggested Reading list), and will do a good deal of reading in back issues of *Liturgical Arts* quarterly. All of these can, however, be profitably and enjoyably read even by those who are not technically trained.

Instead, my purpose is quite limited: to help the "layman" (be he in Holy Orders or not) to understand the changes which he is already meeting and which he is likely to encounter even more in the years just ahead. Given the common level of churches already built in this country, it is un-

131

likely that he will be a regular parishioner in a place where Chapter VII of the Constitution is fully observed. However, many dioceses and parishes are already in the process of rearranging church buildings in line with the Council's directions. And we can hope that this will soon be the case everywhere.

Chapter VII of the Constitution on the Liturgy, "Sacred Art and Sacred Furnishings," is appropriately brief. Its nine articles give only a few but utterly fundamental principles. It is followed, and will be further followed, by more detailed statements issued by the Postconciliar Commission on the Liturgy. Meantime, however, we are happily in possession of an Appendix of suggestions prepared by the Liturgical Preparatory Commission and given to the Fathers of the Council before they voted on the Constitution. Appendix Two of our book is the text of these suggestions. It clearly shows the "mind of the lawgiver" (*mens legislatoris*). Further, since the personnel of the two commissions is very much the same, we are not rash in believing that the directives to come will be very much like those suggested in the Appendix to the Constitution. Thus, I will here use the Appendix to elucidate the meaning of Chapter VII of the Constitution on the Liturgy. (Numbers as indicated from 122 to 130 refer to the Constitution itself; those from 1 to 14 are from the Appendix to the Constitution; those from 90 to 99 are from the first Instruction [Appendix Three of this book], already published by the Postconciliar Commission.)

Historically, the architectural form and scope of the church building has varied widely, from the direct functionalism of the church at Dura-Europos (A.D. 233) through the heavenly majesty of Hagia Sophia, the ecstasy of Chartres, the pomp of St. Peter's and the baroque, to the new efficiency of postwar European structures—to mention just a few important epochs. There are masterpieces to be found in every period, and history makes it plain, as the Constitution says, that "the Church has not adopted any particular style as her very own" (Article 123).

One may be, and indeed one is, expected to have personal preferences, which very likely depend on happy associations or certain favorite moments of history, quite apart from sheer architectural quality. Yet, to belabor the obvious, a church building needs to be judged first in terms of function, as is stressed in the opening sentence of the new Instruction: churches must be "suitable for the celebration of divine services according to the true nature of the services and for the active participation of the faithful" (#90). Thus, whatever else a church may be or do, this basic function must come first and on no account may it be subordinated to other values. Some of these real but secondary values would include: providing a place to retire to for solitude and meditation and private devotion, a rich symbolic structure, an artistic contribution to the urban environment.

These subsidiary functions do have importance. However, history cautions us that they may tend to usurp a primary place. Builders—both clerics and architects—are no more immune to self-glorification than other human beings, and our cities offer dismaying proof of this ingrained trait. A number of worthy pastors have erected structures that were to prove monuments to their personal dedication, always, of course, "for the greater glory of God." And no architect can be expected to aim at less than his best—"best" sometimes meaning virtuosity, imagination, not to mention expensiveness. Not a few churches at all periods (even the "golden" Middle Ages, as Dorothy Sayers brings out in her play about William of Sens, *The Zeal of Thy House*), have transposed the order of values, becoming monumental rather than liturgical, stylish rather than truly functional, exciting and pompous but hardly the house for God's people.

Given the dangers taught us by experience, it seems plain that church-building is too important to be entrusted to any single person. The priest, even if he has read deeply in liturgical theology and continually updated this knowledge by unceasing study, cannot be expected to be an accomplished master of architecture, which is just as demanding and time-consuming a discipline as theology itself. No more can the architect, even if he has read half a dozen books on liturgy, have the sole or final say. The Constitution, thus, urges bishops to "have a special concern for artists, so as to imbue them with the spirit of sacred art and of the sacred liturgy" (Article 127). At the same time, "clerics are to be taught about the history and development of sacred art, and about the sound principles governing the production of its works" (Article 129).

Yet, even when all this has been done, the problem of co-operation will remain and presuppose a large measure of modesty, mutual trust, flexibility and a sense of teamwork.[3]

This is not to say that architects and other artists ought not to be given the greatest freedom and latitude possible. The spirit of the Constitution, Appendix and Instruction is one of enormous openness, with only a bare minimum of restrictions to ensure functionality. It is assumed that builders will absorb and observe the underlying principles and know how to put them into concrete realization. This new open-window policy seems an admission that legalism can be as damaging to liturgical art as is irresponsible individualism. No significant work of art, be it a church or a chant, was ever brought into existence by laws, any more than by lawlessness. If vital liturgical works cannot be unrelated to liturgical needs, neither can they be prefabricated to fit a detailed design. If the artist must check any undue cult of the exclusively personal, the cleric needs to curb a tendency to look for laws even where no laws exist. Juridicism and subjectivism are twin pitfalls. When we judge the Council's reticence, and read the Appendix and Instruction as well, it is plain that our greatest need at present is for Pope John's open-window attitude toward the problem.

Both the Appendix and the Instruction show awareness that we cannot expect existing churches to be torn down. Hence, these documents have a good deal to say about working within these structures, repairing and adapting them to the liturgical needs of the faithful. This requires almost as much—sometimes even more—creativity and a sense of right order as does a new building. Where an ornate altar, reredos and retable included, is already there, it is obviously inappropriate for the "altar of sacrifice" to be devoid of dignity and "noble beauty" (Article 124). Thus, the work of adaptation should by no means be whimsical, random or makeshift, but assumes the skill of a liturgically alert architect.

Models of how not to proceed are legion. Among models of successful procedure, surely one of the most eminent is that of the Cathedral of Cuernavaca, where a baroque (indeed, Churrigueresque) structure was adapted to contemporary style by the co-operative efforts of an enlightened bishop working with a team of top-flight liturgists, architects and other artists. Our problems in North America should be somewhat less acute than in Latin countries, where exuberant altar screens and grilles (obstructing any sense of participation) are often structural elements of the building and are thus hard to remove. But in most cases here in North America any careful change will mean no loss.

If, however, a new church is to be built (and with our

nomadic trend toward exurbia and suburbia there is every reason to believe that this will be increasingly the case), the general lines of development are clear. The church is to be centered on the altar of sacrifice—separated from the wall, as both the Instruction (#91) and the Appendix (#3) make explicit, and occupying a place "which is truly central" (#91). Central, however, does not necessarily imply the so-called "church in the round," with the altar literally in the middle. The problem of an ideal shape for the liturgical building has been much discussed in the literature on the subject. It is well summed up in Father Kevin Seasoltz's volume *Sacred Art and Architecture,* and in a full issue of *La Maison-Dieu* (No. 63, 1960), both of which should be studied by anyone interested in pursuing the whole topic. Perhaps the most celebrated instance of a completely circular church in this country is that of the St. Louis Priory. There the altar is not placed in the very center. Nor, of course, was it generally so placed in the central-plan structures that were so common in the Byzantine era. For, though a strict centering may symbolize the communitarian aspect of the Church and the centrality of the altar, it neglects other aspects of the mystery, like the hierarchical structure of the Church and its teaching function.

The altar facing the people is now explicitly permitted (Instruction, #95). Many priests and people were strenuously opposed to this on principle before experiencing it, but have been converted after a short time. Granted that it complicates and calls attention to certain problems: the number of signs of the cross and certain other gestures during the Canon, for example. There is also a question of reducing some of the sense of mystery and transcendence at Mass, the "vertical" aspect, the sacral.[4] The advantages of clarity, however, clearly outweigh whatever loss is sustained. The sense of participation is notably heightened, and the active participation insisted on by the Constitution is enormously facilitated by this arrangement.

Further, there are ways of compensating for any loss of the sense of awe. For one thing, the priest can become much more careful about his manner of speaking and gesticulating. Certain architectural features, such as spacing and lighting, can balance off any disadvantage. The "sufficient size" called for by the Instruction (#91) can be made impressive enough to suggest a fitting distance, without the loss of a correlative sense of closeness. This is, obviously, not a matter for minute regulation, but is one that must be solved by an architect who understands all the demands of liturgy, and possesses the sensitivity and control of space to bring this about concretely.

A further problem occurs in the reservation of the Blessed Sacrament. No responsible liturgist, to my knowledge, would suggest a return to the first thousand years of the Church, when the Blessed Sacrament was reserved only for Communion to the sick; too precious are the gains in devotion for us to turn back. At the same time, the somewhat over-developed stress on reservation, to the neglect of the more strictly sacrificial and sacramental uses of the Eucharist, during a number of centuries, calls for a shift in emphasis. Here the comparative silence of the Constitution is eloquent, and it would be fanciful to suppose it was unintentional. For the Constitution mentions the tabernacle only once (Article 128), when providing for an early revision of liturgical laws, which are to treat of "the nobility, placing, and safety of the Eucharistic tabernacle."

Both the Appendix and the Instruction, however, suggest several solutions. The tabernacle should be either on the main altar, or on a minor "but truly outstanding altar"

(Instruction, #95), or "in some other noble and properly adorned part of the church." The Appendix (Appendix, #6) suggests that greater reverence might be secured if there is a "special chapel of the Eucharist." There remains the problem of relating the tabernacle to the altar of sacrifice, for both theological and practical reasons—as, for example, when not enough Hosts have been consecrated at a given Mass and it is necessary to use Hosts from the tabernacle.

There are liturgists who prefer the Blessed Sacrament chapel for theological reasons. Put simply, it seems psychologically more sound to keep the mystery of the sacrifice-banquet visually distinct from that of reservation, since people may become confused and find it hard to concentrate on the given action. The Mass is the worship of the Father by the Son, in Whom we are incorporated and with Whom we share in worship. The Blessed Sacrament is the worship of Christ our Lord by us. Accordingly, it may be said that it is more suitable to have these two distinct acts and loci of worship clearly and visually distinct. Needless to say, at present liturgists are not in perfect agreement on the architectural expression best adapted to our present needs. Thus we many expect the new freedom to lead to new and interesting solutions. And since, after all, uniformity of practice is by no means always a desirable thing, great riches may well be the upshot of such diversity. (For many examples of such possible solutions, see the recent issue of *L'Art d'Eglise*, No. 130.)

The other important focus of attention at Mass has to do with the proclamation of the Word and the prayers before the beginning of the Offertory. Here several objects become visually significant: the seat of the celebrant and the ambo or lectern. The celebrant's chair (Appendix, #2, and Instruction, #92) must be "so placed that it may be easily seen by the faithful and that the celebrant may truly appear to preside over the entire community of the faithful." The new instructions for the Mass keep the altar for the strictly Eucharistic part of the Mass; thus, the celebrant performs his presidential function at a chair (not a throne, unless he is a bishop), which symbolizes his leadership in the prayer of the Church.

The ambo or lectern is discussed briefly (Appendix, #7, and Instruction, #96). It is to be so arranged that the ministers (deacon, subdeacon and, in their absence, priest or other reader) "can be easily seen and heard by the faithful." Only one ambo is mentioned in the Instruction, and this seems desirable for several reasons: one is not to clutter up the sacred area with unnecessary objects; another is to stress the unity of the Word of God (whether Epistle, Gospel, Old Testament lesson, or homily).[5]

Another noteworthy change called for by the Constitution, and further emphasized by both Instruction and Appendix, has to do with minor altars, statues and other images. As we have just seen, the number of images "should be moderate and their relative positions should reflect right order" (Article 125). The reason given has to do with theology—"otherwise they may create confusion among the Christian people and foster devotion of doubtful orthodoxy." Thus, as should be self-evident, images of Christ should be given the highest importance, and "the multiplication of . . . images behind the main altar is altogether disapproved of" (Appendix, #12). Further, minor altars "shall be few in number, [and] it is highly suitable that they be placed in chapels in some way separated from the principal part of the church" (Instruction, #93). Again, we are in an area of psychological economy: our human ability to concentrate on few things at once; the good can often be "the enemy of the better." And since most of our churches, far from following the ancient and medieval example of Rome (where no statues were used in church), have tended to be overadorned with images, at least for the time being we would do well to follow Father Godfrey Diekmann's suggestion to "be prudently and orthodoxally iconoclastic." [6]

This is not to be interpreted as downgrading or abandoning sculpture, stained glass, painting or other arts within the church. Rather the contrary. It opens new possibilities to the creativity of really imaginative artists. After all, the altar, if it is to show that it is a symbol of Christ and the place of the paschal sacrifice-banquet, requires the most gifted and liturgically grounded treatment. Its size and proportions, too, are most important both in terms of function and symbolism, and will require great craftsmanship. The same holds for the ambo, the presidential seat, the place for Communion (Communion "Stations," instead of rails, are a new—and ancient—development which will call for fresh handling, the rails being less satisfactory as suggesting too great a rift between the altar and the priestly people of God). Baptistries and confessionals call for visual treatment that will satisfy both symbolic and practical needs (Appendix, #10 and #11).

Very wisely, the Constitution makes no legislation on the matter of styles, save to deny that there is any one style and to welcome modern art (Article 123). Since, again, there is no such thing as a single valid modern expression, the utmost in responsible freedom is called for here. The Appendix explicitly welcomes both "decorative and iconographic" art, urging that we "always seek a balance between the two, as well as between the realistic and the abstract" (#13). It is

incontrovertible, I believe, that the altar crucifix should
be at least somewhat representational, whereas windows and
much other ornamentation will give wider scope to various
types of abstraction and symbolism. The many naturalistic
horrors that proliferated in most nineteenth- and early-twen-
tieth-century churches in the name of "tradition" are a scandal
and should serve us with warnings.[7]

Another great need today is for more attention to be paid
to several arts which, precisely because their products are
not as large or irremovable as those already mentioned, are
often shockingly neglected. Not only do vestments offer
scope for abstract creativeness, but so do metalwork, wood-
work, tapestry and rug design, as well as other work in cloth.
Indeed, anything that is visual, from missals to candlesticks,
calls for serious artistic competence and a liturgically
developed sense. Variety to fit the seasons and feasts can
be attained by the use of abstract or representational tapes-
tries and banners. It would be unfortunate indeed if contemporary or modern were allowed to mean "sterile, cold,
disinfected."

In this connection, certain mottoes of distinguished artistic
innovators must be taken, not in isolation as though they
represented a complete artistic credo, but in terms of the
abuses that they were designed to correct, or specific problems to be solved. Thus, to define a church as "a machine
to live in" does less than justice to the great creative architect who coined the phrase. The same may be said of "form
follows function," "form is function," "less is more," and the
like. A certain cleanness, sense of order and function, even
sparseness and a measure of austerity, should not imply the
absence of warmth, color or human feeling.

It would be well if all artists and persons concerned about

religion and art came to know Father P.-R. Régamey's masterly work *Religious Art in the Twentieth Century,* which is surely a *summa* of sound artistic sense and openness.

Music

Music's position among the liturgical arts is at once privileged, precarious and endlessly exposed to criticism. There is, as I write this, a fairly broad ground swell of antipathy to the "new liturgical music." Some of this is occasioned by the loss of "old favorites," and while most of these old favorites were not of great quality, there is no doubt that no one likes to see the Palestrina settings of the Ordinary go into oblivion. Strictly speaking, the Constitution says nothing about abandoning these works, good or mediocre: the sentimental, residually romantic hymns and Masses are being eliminated on the grounds of good sense and the greater sophistication of today's priests and people; the great works were performed in few places, and continue to be performed in most of these places. Thus, the anguish is really not as seriously founded as might be supposed.

At the same time, music is privileged. The Constitution devotes a whole chapter to it, and praises its tradition as "a treasure of inestimable value, greater even than that of any other art." Yet, musicians should not take undue pride, or nonmusicians undue umbrage, at this, for the reason is instantly added: "as sacred song united to the words, it forms a necessary or integral part of the solemn liturgy" (Article 112).

Thus, the discussion here is not on an abstract aesthetic plane, as though music were somehow "purer" than the other arts—whatever that silly encomium may be intended to mean. Its eminence is based on something forthright and

142

unambiguous: whereas the other arts provide the setting for the liturgy, music enters directly into the very words used by the people of God. Nothing, be it noted, is said about poetry in the liturgy, or about the dance (in the most embracing sense of the term, to include the rather stylized gestures made by priest and people).

The Constitution next speaks of the "ministerial function" of music, its role in the service of God and God's people at worship. While this is not spelled out in detail, three "ministries" are mentioned: "it adds delight to prayer, fosters unity of minds, or confers greater solemnity upon the sacred rites." (I am not altogether happy about this standard translation of *orationem suavius exprimens* as "adds delight to prayer," though it roughly expresses the thought.)

There is nothing puritanical here, or narrowly utilitarian. Further, the Constitution immediately affirms that "the Church approves of all forms of true art having the needed qualities, and admits them into divine worship." Only a single gentle but firm reminder is added: "the purpose of sacred music . . . is the glory of God and the sanctification of the faithful."

We are thus plunged into the realm of tension, so inescapable in any discussion of the Church or liturgy. It is no secret that very often "professional liturgists" and "professional musicians" have had some difficulty getting along together. While the former tend to "keep music in its place," the latter rightly insist that music is an art and must enjoy some autonomy if it is to be true music. This human tension, with all its implied theoretical roots, cannot be easily resolved; still less should it be simply covered over as though non-existent or too hopeless to acknowledge.[8]

If the ministry of music were restricted to expressing the glory of God, while the congregation participated only by listening and appreciating, the problem would be simpler, though still difficult enough, thanks to the widely diverse standards of taste and training among the listeners. While some listeners would be uplifted by the *B-Minor Mass,* others would find it easier to be moved by Gounod's *St. Caecilia Mass,* and yet others would be quite satisfied with the derivative Yon-Montani type, and so on down the scale toward unplumbed depths.

This is altogether apart from the problems arising out of totally different cultures—East and West, for example. Where *Missa Luba* (which is, of course, not by any means purely African), *Missa Bantu* (which is even less so) and Joseph Kyagambiddwa's enchanting and authentic work (say, his *Uganda Martyrs African Oratorio*) strike Westerners as exotic or quaint, the response of Africans is presumably quite different, and contingent on their degree of westernization. In any case, the often quoted adage that music is the international language, however applicable within the area of nations united by a fairly common culture, is grotesquely false when we try to apply it between unrelated cultures. There, music is found to be, if anything, the most impenetrable and uncommunicative of the traditional arts. Most people find it far easier to "understand" Chinese painting, for example, or Indian and African and New Hebridean sculpture, than to make anything of the music from those cultural areas.

Again, if the ministry of music were simply one of providing the plainest, most singable vehicle for common participation, with no thought given to aesthetic quality, the problem would disappear. But at an enormous price. The most pedestrian hymn may serve for a time, and may even prove inoffensive to large parts of an average congregation. Yet it quickly reveals its vacuity. Nor does it fill man's felt need for

144

at least some beauty in worship. Nor, for that matter, does it comply with the Constitution's insistence on "true art" and the "more noble form" of liturgy when sung (Article 112, 113), still less on "the treasure of sacred music . . . to be preserved and fostered with great care" (Article 114). Musical minimalism cannot be the solution. Nor can the principle: if it's bland and dull it's liturgical, and the blander and duller, the more liturgical.

The entire tone of the Constitution's chapter on sacred music is unmistakable: "The musical tradition of the universal Church is a treasure of inestimable value" (#112). It is not as though music were grudgingly admitted into worship, for "Holy Scripture, indeed, has bestowed praise upon sacred song, and the same may be said of the fathers of the Church." (Granted that many of the glowing things said by the Fathers of the Church applied only to psalm singing. We find, for example, St. Gregory of Nyssa telling of his sister St. Macrina that she sang "when rising from bed, or when taking up serious matters or recreating, going to meals or leaving the table." Even ordinary Christians, he says, "wayfarers, sailors, or men that spend their days at the workbench—all men and women in every occupation, in sickness and in health, sang the psalms and canticles of the Church." [9]

Further, if the Constitution's tonality is bright, its modality is "major" and cheerful. As elsewhere in the document, the Council seemed determined to affirm rather than to deny, to open rather than to close. What few restrictions appear come under the form of positive approval of something else. Nothing is explicitly condemned.

This mood reflects, I believe, more than a general optimism consonant with Pope John's personality and hopes. The Council Fathers, or whoever drafted the Constitution's text, must have been aware of the bankruptcy brought on by some sixty years of a largely negative approach. True, St. Pius X's great motu proprio of 1903, taken as a whole, contains much that is affirmative. Yet, in the anxious mood of the Modernist crisis that bedeviled his pontificate, certain cautionary or even inquisitorial forces went to work zealously to purge church music of its worldliness. Societies that were set up, often enough self-appointed, to raise standards of sacred music eliminated more than they created. Heroic groups, like Manhattanville's Pius X School of Music, did miracles in the performance of Gregorian chant and medieval and Renaissance polyphony—probably surpassing in perfection anything ever accomplished while these musical forms were actually being created. Certain monasteries, seminaries, cathedrals and exceptional parishes offered sacred music that meant something to their members and proved an object of admiration to musically inclined visitors. I recall, while studying at Solesmes Abbey, meeting Protestants, Jews, agnostics and even a Buddhist or two, who came there to hear Gregorian chant impressively performed in an appropriate setting, and even to draw inspiration for their own work back at home. It would be ungracious and short of the truth to underestimate the quality of sacred music there, and at Quarr Abbey, Saint-Wandrille, Saint-Benoît-du-Lac, En-Calcat and a dozen other places, largely monastic, where I have been privileged to hear it. Yet, sad to say, the overwhelming majority of Catholics in Europe and America have never known the joy of worshiping in musical beauty.

Further, again with the exception of certain monasteries and a few other privileged institutions, even when musical beauty was present its function often seemed more akin to that of incense, or to a stained-glass atmosphere, or as a backdrop to meditation, than to what the present Constitution envisions. For its insistence is rather on "the active participation of the people" (Article 113), "the whole body of the faithful [contributing] that active participation which is rightly theirs" (Article 114), "religious singing by the people," the voices of the faithful ringing out (Article 118), "the active participation of the entire assembly of the faithful" (Article 121). The theme is reiterated, much as the subject of a monothematic fugue.

However, as we examine the document more closely we detect another theme, running along in insistent counterpoint. The Constitution nowhere says that all liturgical music must be sung only by the congregation as a whole. Rather the contrary. "Choirs must be diligently promoted" (Article 114); "other kinds of sacred music, especially polyphony, are by no means excluded from liturgical celebrations" (Article 116); "the pipe organ is to be held in high esteem, . . . but other instruments also may be admitted for use in divine worship" (Article 120); composers are invited to provide not only "works which can be sung only by large choirs," but should provide also for the needs of small choirs (Article 121). Thus, the Constitution's fugue is by no means monothematic, but contains a countersubject of almost equal importance in the total texture.

Cynics will easily assert, of course, that the document is a pastiche, a compromise, and that a skilled specialist in form-criticism could identify and isolate the individual authors or schools of authors whose work went into it. This analysis, while appealing and facile enough, falls short of the reality, and bypasses the more fundamental fact and obvious explanation. It is that music has more than one function in liturgy.

This should not prove surprising given the wider principle of distinction of roles in the Church and her worship.

For the Mystical Body is not homogenized, a sort of un-differentiated blob of protoplasm, but an articulated, or-dered, organic reality. The Constitution on the Church is quite explicit regarding this truth: "Christ the Lord in-stituted in His Church a variety of ministries which work for the good of the whole body" (Article 18). It goes on to describe the ministry of service of bishops and priests, with their specific tasks, liturgical and otherwise. The Constitu-tion on the Sacred Liturgy (Articles 26–30) makes it abun-dantly clear that different members of the Church share in the priestly and liturgical work in different ways, whether as bishop, priest, server, lector, commentator or as members of the choir, who "also exercise a genuine liturgical func-tion" (Article 29).

This is made even more explicit in the new instruction on celebrating Mass (the *Ordo Missae*) now in force. Here the distinction of roles is emphasized; the priest performs only his own function, the people theirs, the choir theirs.

However, it must be admitted that the line of demarcation between music that belongs strictly to the people and music that belongs to the choir is not always precise. It is an oversimplification to say that the Ordinary belongs to the people and the Proper to the choir. For the choir also be-longs to the people, and though historically it has usurped the people's role and at some times in the past needed to be "cut down to size," it is still very much needed today, and perhaps always will be, to guide, support and hearten the people.

Further, as Archabbot Rembert Weakland put it suc-cinctly: "There has never been a time in the Church when the people sang the Proper in its entirety as we know it. The faithful never sang the Gradual and Alleluia, the Tract and the Sequences. The same can be said of the Introit and Offertory. If these are to become people's chants, in whole or in part, they must change radically in character. They must become simple antiphons or hymns." [10] Even if this should come about—and the suggestion seems most appropriate, since they and the Communion are meant to be processional and popular in character—there is still a place for music for contemplation during the Mass.

During the moments of meditation following the Epistle we need time, a climate for recollection and response to God's Word. It seems most fitting for the choir to sing during the moments after Communion, as well as during recessionals and before the official Introit. There need be no conflict, no unilateral and exclusive dedication to one or the other. In fact, a number of churches where I have found participation most developed are also known for the excellence of their choirs.

Another great open-door gesture made by the Constitution is in favor of composers. They are invited to "feel that their vocation is to cultivate sacred music and increase its store of treasures" (Article 121). Again the mood is one of authentic welcome and not of mere toleration. Nor do we find lists of inhibiting restrictions set down.

Only two limits are drawn, both eminently reasonable: the music for the liturgy shall have the "qualities proper to genuine sacred music" and the texts to be sung must be "in conformity with Catholic doctrine; indeed they should be drawn chiefly from holy scripture and from liturgical sources." Surely no composer will find this unconscionably cramping.

Further, there is the very practical plea for compositions that are not only suitable to large choirs, but for small choirs as well, and for the active participation of the faithful. One of the lamentable traits of Catholic liturgical music for some centuries is its tendency to be either difficult or worthless. It is hard to name a single Mass or body of motets composed in recent centuries that has musical value which is not technically beyond the capacity of most choirs and congregations. Magnificent as the Stravinsky and Křenek Masses doubtless are, they require performing resources that make them totally inaccessible to any but a rare choir in this country. The few exceptions that come to mind (say, some of the Poulenc motets, the Stravinsky *Pater* and *Ave,* and a minuscule number of others) stand out by reason of their rarity.

Meantime, while the significant composers of the last century or so have been either repelled, or at least discouraged through lack of commissions or scant prospects of performance, our market of sacred music has been flooded with a tide of *Kitsch,* whose main merit is its conformity to negative regulations. Not long ago I participated in judging a contest of sacred music in which it proved hard conscientiously to choose a composition deserving of reward. One of the jurors happened to be among the world's most respected critics. His comments, after he had examined the submitted compositions (which had already been filtered by a previous committee), were as follows: "primitive," "watered-down Franck," "clichés," "unconvincingly pretentious," "organist's rambling," "pseudo-modality," "a Regerish play with chromaticism," "Puccini brought up to date," and the like. His appended note apologized for lack of experience "with this particular species of composer" and with "the hinterland from which this music comes." I was painfully reminded of Gilson's great phrase: "Piety does not dispense with technique."

Several years ago, before the Council completed its Constitution on the Sacred Liturgy, Igor Stravinsky very gener-

ously granted me an interview.[11] Mr. Stravinsky found the
present state of Catholic liturgical music "corrupt, appalling, disgraceful." The only solution, as he saw it, was "to
clean out the whole thing—all those conservative idiots who
keep the standards of sacred music down at zero—those
composers who serve up the same old clichés rehashed!" If
this were done, and the vernacular allowed, he foresaw the
possible rise of "a new golden age in Church music."

To admit that such a golden age is not yet with us, or
even on the verge of coming about (barring some miracle
of musical alchemy), should cause no argument. No one is
more sadly aware of our present plight than serious, sensi-
tive musicians, people who have dedicated a lifetime and
much talent to a largely thankless service. Today, particularly, whenever the Constitution has been interpreted as
restrictively as possible, musicians in many parishes feel
deeply frustrated and thwarted at every turn. They are told
all the things they may not do, but are given little help as
to concrete possibilities. Thus, a number of highly qualified
artists have felt coerced into abandoning sacred music,
sometimes after years of service.

Church music can be expected to reach, if not a golden,
at least an honest bronze age, only if it is taken seriously.
The problem lies, it need hardly be said, not with the
Constitution, but with the selective, largely negative reading
of that great and liberating document. As long as choir-
masters are paid smaller wages than janitors, and given
considerably less elbow room, they can hardly be expected
to produce music worthy of God or God's people.

The same sort of problem that exists in the architect-
pastor relationship is found in the musician-pastor relationship. Neither partner must dominate; each must be
sufficiently instructed in the other's métier and respectful

of the other's professional competence to make the partnership fruitful. Lines of a solution are suggested by the Constitution: "Great importance is to be attached to the teaching and practice of music in seminaries" (Article 115). If this is done with the seriousness that a decree of an Ecumenical Council merits, we may hope someday to have priests sufficiently trained to be able to communicate with musicians and presumably informed enough to know their personal limitations.

At the same time, the Constitution assumes that musicians will be "filled with the Christian spirit" (Article 121), and that they will understand the liturgical implications of their truly "ministerial function" (Article 112). In this day of widespread liturgical interest and with the abundance of literature available and the excellent opportunities for liturgical and musical training, in both a growing number of dioceses and first-class summer schools at a truly professional level, we have no reason to despair.

The major area of hope, however, is in today's children, who will be trained in hymns that are within their comprehension yet not insulting to the adult intelligence. The enormous amount of energy that went into teaching young children difficult works, in a tongue they did not understand, had no proportionate results. As soon as we have a good supply of English Masses of respectable musical quality, there is no reason why the young generation cannot quickly learn them and provide leadership for the older among us. Thus, our music teachers have the key to the future.

The Constitution offers a bridge, too, to link the liturgists and musicians who traditionally were separated by a chasm of opposing interests. Since the Constitution has appeared, it seems that we meet fewer and fewer extremists. Musicians

seem increasingly informed on the true meaning of liturgy
and their part in it, while liturgists show more awareness
of the Church's need for qualified musicians. From both
sides, more and more dedicated persons seem willing and
eager to help in the selfless task of bridge-building, in the
spirit of the Constitution. True, even theoretical problems
remain—such as the role of Gregorian chant, which the
Constitution mentions briefly: "other things being equal,
it should be given pride of place in liturgical services" (Article 116). (No one seems to know precisely what these
phrases mean.) We are fortunate to have a serious, balanced treatment of the whole subject of sacred music in
Father Joseph Gelineau's volume, *Voices and Instruments
in Christian Worship* (now available in English), and his
brief chapter, "The Role of Sacred Music," and that of
Helmut Hucke, "Church Music," in the recent Concilium
volume: *The Church and the Liturgy*. Both musicians and
nonmusicians ought to study these works, to find the best
of commentaries on the Council's brief treatment.

The subject of liturgical music is, thus, neither simple
nor unimportant. Perhaps nowhere in our liturgical renewal
must greater flexibility and a range of freedom and experimentation be allowed. For music, in order to be functional, must be constantly related to the people whom it is
to serve—the individual congregation or group, with varying
levels of age, cultural sophistication, background. Music
suitable for one group may prove not as suitable for another. Here trained judgment, rather than a multiplicity of
regulations, is called for. There can be no pat formulas, at
least not at our present stage of growth.

At the moment, and presumably for the next few years
during which a great deal of trial and error together with
some heartbreak will be our lot, the pressing need is for

good participational music: Masses, hymns, psalmody and other congregational material. However, it would not be amiss for all who have something to do with church music, pastors or musicians, to keep an eye constantly on Article 8 in the Constitution, which has not often been quoted, but which may keep our sights and spirits high:

"In the earthly liturgy we take part in a foretaste of that heavenly liturgy which is celebrated in the holy city of Jerusalem toward which we journey as pilgrims, where Christ is sitting at the right hand of God, a minister of the holies and of the true tabernacle; we sing a hymn to the Lord's glory with all the warriors of the heavenly army; venerating the memory of the saints, we hope for some part and fellowship with them; we eagerly await the Savior, our Lord Jesus Christ, until He, our life, shall appear and we too will appear with Him in glory."

With no false triumph or vulgar ostentation, and remembering that we "journey as pilgrims," we need some visual and musical reminders of the heavenly liturgy which we are anticipating. Music and the other sacred arts offer just the touch of joy and heavenly glow, even here on earth, that all of us at times hunger for, especially when we gather as the people of God in praise of God.

EIGHT

Anxieties About the Liturgy

$\mathcal{T}$he Constitution contains at least one caution, which is not, as a cynic might be tempted to suggest, simply a case of taking back with one hand what has been given with the other. It comes in Article 9, early in Chapter I: "The sacred liturgy does not exhaust the entire activity of the Church."

To pretend that, simply because "the liturgy is the summit toward which the activity of the Church is directed" and "the fount from which all her power flows" (Article 10), and that everything somehow becomes liturgy, is to deprive the word of any clear content. In his thought-provoking commentary, *The Liturgy Revived,* Father Louis Bouyer develops this point at some length: "The liturgy must not be made everything, which would be equivalent to making it simply anything." For even in theology, good fences are needed.

The Constitution goes on to give a healthy reminder that in order for the liturgy to be able "to produce its full effects, it is necessary that the faithful come to it with proper dispositions, that their minds should be attuned to their voices, and they should cooperate with divine grace lest they receive it in vain" (Article 11).

One of the counterfeits of religion which pious men have always had to beware of is the desire to find shortcuts or panaceas. This sometimes takes the form of magic, or the attempt to control supernatural power or mana. The human instinct for security, not to mention the will to power, may easily tend to covet such control. We recurrently encounter the mania for "signs and wonders," the cult of prescience (or prophecy in the narrow sense of foretelling the future and thereby somehow gaining a certain possession of it) in certain religious sects and even in some of the enthusiasm for the "letter of Fatima" (which was to be opened in 1960, and from which devotees expected detailed apocalyptic directives). Much of the present craze for hallucinogenic or psychodelic drugs is a manifestation of this same drive for prophetic powers.

Liturgy, as we know it in the Church, is of course as far removed as possible from any religious eccentricity. The sober, structured, Roman ethos of our Latin rite has, in fact, been an antidote to mere enthusiasm. If anything, it may be charged with thwarting or leaving too little scope for the charismatic impulse. Yet, in another way, enthusiasm for liturgy has its own hazards: it may, in fact, lead to exaggerated expectations, with subsequent disenchantment.

In one of the truly significant works of our time, *Christ, the Sacrament of the Encounter with God,* Father Edward Schillebeeckx devotes a final chapter to "The Mystical Quality of the Sacraments." With perfect candor he warns that "we are bound to come sharply up against the experience that, however basically sincere our desire for grace and however genuine our trust in God may be, the resultant effects in our active Christian life do not, despite frequent good moments, really measure up completely to our desire for grace or our trust in God." He then makes a specifically liturgical application: "It is a common human experience that the frequent reception of the sacraments does not always result in a mature Christian life."

The problem is real and not susceptible to quick solution; rather than pretend to summarize Father Schillebeeckx's answer, let me urge my readers to read or reread at least this wonderful chapter mentioned above. Liturgy, even the renewed liturgy, and any conceivable liturgy that would incorporate all our desires, can never be used as a pretext for externalism, or the escape from the selfless effort at sincerity, generosity, acceptance and openness to God's initiative. For, to quote Schillebeeckx again, "God's love is always greater than ours, and His grace always transcends our personal religious attitude," and further, "however sincere the Christian's disposition may be, he cannot keep up with this grace, which constantly goes ahead of him."

The Constitution further cautions us that the "spiritual life . . . is not by any means limited solely to participation in the liturgy. The Christian is indeed called to pray with his brethren, but he must also enter into his chamber to pray to the Father in secret; yet more, according to the teaching of the Apostle, he should pray without ceasing" (Article 12). Thus, liturgy, properly understood, is no substitute for contemplation or even—in the Christian not the Stoic or Pelagian sense—asceticism. The Christian life, and real liturgical participation too, make stern demands. The Christian's response to God's Word and his identification with Christ's redemptive work can never mean less than commitment.

True, our century has developed the special awareness that emerges from dialogue and group dynamics, and this

valuable discovery is well co-ordinated with liturgical attitudes. Yet there remains another type of awareness that is
no less profoundly human and Christian. Since we are
human beings, and not exclusively gregarious creatures, our
consciousness is not collective but personal. Thus, we need
to withdraw from society to "pray to the Father in secret,"
as our Lord Himself did. We need periods of retreat into
ourselves, for reflection in depth, for personal encounter
with God. While we remain social beings, we are not social
all of the time in the same way. Even within the liturgical
action there should be time for personal prayer—not in-
dulged in with a "Jesus-and-I-alone" attitude, but nevertheless in silence. There is such a thing as holy silence right
at the heart of liturgy. At present it is provided by the
silent recitation of the Canon. However, when the Canon
is said aloud, as we may foresee with some likelihood (there
are experimental provisions for this already), some moments
should be provided for liturgical silence.

In our ongoing adjustments of the practices of worship,
the last thing in the world that anyone wants is some new
externalism, which could prove as sterile as the very things
in the process of being remedied. One of the thinkers who
have most influenced present liturgical thinking, Odo Casel,
left us this reminder: "With the liturgy, the decisive thing
is inward participation, which does not require uncondition-
ally to be made external." However, he quickly added: "But
external participation does belong to the intense sharing
of the experience, and to the completion of its symbolic
expression." After all, or before all, we are embodied, not
detached, spirits.[1]

Another possible liturgical pitfall, which may seem quite
removed from the extremism just mentioned but which is
no less escapist in fact, is that of lapsing into a new jurid-

icism. There are those who, in panicky flight from the responsibility of freedom, persist in wanting everything neatly and meticulously legislated. The healthy opposite of chaos is not total regimentation but maturity. To want every gesture, prayer or church appointment to be controlled in minute detail may look like the perfection of obedience, but may more likely be only a form of spiritual sloth. Some people do find it easier to be treated as puppets than as persons.

An unavowed presupposition of this view is that inflexible uniformity is always the better thing. Accustomed as we have long been to being told exactly where the tabernacle should be, what material it should be made of, how many inches apart the priest's hands should be held, in what order candles should be lighted and extinguished, we may find the new opportunity for responsible experimentation and adaptation a challenging, if not a frightening, experience. We are going through a kind of collective adolescence, during this period of change, and some of us may be attracted by the thought of golden childhood or the cozy womb. The present "unstuck" situation of the liturgy is far from comfortable.

Such faith in regulations and rubrics—"Let's have anything, so long as it doesn't change again or isn't different in different places"—may be the most insidious liturgical temptation of this moment. It takes humility to accept the fact that we are not at the end of change, but very much in a moment of transition; that many of our current changes can only be tentative and exploratory; that a future generation will look back on our efforts as gauche, or at best naïve though well intentioned. Like Faust we wish to perpetuate the precious moment, freeze it, impose it on the future. If we take this approach, we may end up with a

159

diminished liturgy rather than a renewed one, and this would surely be the furthest thing from the intention of the Council.

Father Frederick R. McManus, a foremost liturgist and expert at the Council, points to the "definite break with the traditional pattern of rigid, precise rubrical directions" in favor of "choices, alternatives, variations." Thus, he explains, "much is left to the judgment and responsibility of the individual pastor and celebrant." Granted, "the new flexibility places a burden on the priest, who must study and plan how to satisfy the needs of the community of worshipers over whom he presides." [2] Much of this burden, I should add, lies on the laity too, notably on those who are liturgically well instructed—sometimes better than those who preside over them.

Article 13 of the Constitution adds another caution against too individualistic an interpretation of liturgical devotions: "Popular devotions of the Christian people are to be highly commended, provided they accord with the laws and norms of the Church, above all when they are ordered by the Apostolic See." And the same is said about local devotions, if they are controlled by the bishop.

This should allay anxieties of many devout Catholics—and not by any means only among the simple and uninstructed—regarding anything like a wholesale abandonment of what is surely a part of Christian tradition. Articles 103 and 104 remind us to honor with special love the Blessed Virgin, Mother of God, and to celebrate the passage of the saints from earth to heaven. For in Mary we admire "the most excellent fruit of the redemption," while in the saints "the Church proclaims the paschal mystery achieved in the saints who have suffered and been glorified with Christ."

This theme is further developed in Chapters VII and

VIII of the Constitution on the Church. What is particularly noteworthy about these chapters is not, as is sometimes rashly asserted by people who have never bothered to read them, that the Blessed Virgin and the saints are "downgraded," but rather that their role and our corresponding attitudes are *situated* within the total context of the redemption.

The value of this precise theological focus will be granted by anyone who has traveled in countries where Catholic education is notoriously underdeveloped, and where the peripheral has often the appearance of the central—which is not to say that theologically grounded devotion to Mary and the saints is at all peripheral. On this subject, the rhetorical excesses of certain contributors to the sensational volume *Objections to Roman Catholicism* should not blind us to the fact that devotional eccentricities do exist and do call for remedy.

Chapter VII of the Constitution on the Church deals with "The Eschatological Nature of the Pilgrim Church and Its Union With the Church in Heaven"—a formidable, meaningful title. It sees the saints as more closely united with Christ. Through Him and with Him and in Him they do not cease to intercede with the Father for us, "showing forth the merits which they won on earth through the one Mediator between God and man." In the saints, God vividly "manifests His presence and His face to men; He speaks to us in them and gives us a sign of His Kingdom, to which we are strongly drawn, having so great a cloud of witness over us and such a witness to the truth of the Gospel" (cf. Hebrews 12:1).

The Council refers to possible "abuses, excesses or defects" in devotion to the saints, and urges the faithful to learn the "authentic cult" of the saints, which consists not

161

so much in multiplying external acts, but rather in the greater intensity of our love. We are to seek from the saints "example in their way of life, fellowship in their communion and aid by their intercession."

Chapter VIII, "The Blessed Virgin Mary, Mother of God, in the Mystery of Christ and the Church," honors her as endowed with the high office and dignity of being the Mother of the Son of God. The true theological perspective is clearly shown: "At the same time, because she belongs to the offspring of Adam she is one with all those who are to be saved, a pre-eminent and singular member of the Church, and its type and excellent exemplar in faith and charity." Accordingly, the Council promotes devotion to Mary, "especially the liturgical cult," while exhorting "theologians and preachers of the divine Word to abstain zealously both from all false exaggerations as well as from too great narrowness of mind" in their Marian devotion, but always to keep the focus on Christ, "the source of all truth, holiness and piety."

This entire chapter, the final one on the Church, is a model of liturgical, Scriptural, kerygmatic theology. Its balance and restraint and centrality should do a great deal to eliminate excesses in both directions: either toward a Mariology dissociated from Christology, or toward a somewhat puritanical Mariaphobia, or, in the case of the saints, hagiophobia.

There still remains the problem of application. For, as Nocent put it, "the human psyche cannot be indefinitely strained"; we cannot concentrate on everything at once. Hence, the importance of achieving proportion. It is not a question of abandoning our devotions, but of relating them.

The Constitution on the Liturgy offers several clues about how to relate these devotions to their theological center. Article 103 places the liturgical honor given to Mary precisely within the "annual cycle of Christ's mysteries." The Marian feasts are thus commemorations of Christ's own redemptive work and anticipations of His ultimate victory. Another hint is given in Chapter VII, which deals with sacred art: it insists on moderation in images and right order, lest they "foster devotion of doubtful orthodoxy." [3]

Devotions that more explicitly relate to our Lord Himself have also their liturgical stress. Father Jungmann has suggested that the feast of the Sacred Heart (appropriately always on a Friday) is a sort of Good Friday "seen from within." Granted that many of the trappings surrounding this devotion are anachronistic relics of bygone art and vocabulary, and even calculated to repel the theologically sophisticated Christian of today. Yet it is interesting to note that Karl Rahner has devoted a great number of profound pages to the Sacred Heart devotion and finds it singularly meaningful for our time—a time which he describes as one of Diaspora—of dispersion—for the Church.

Understood as the personal commitment to Christ in His redemptive work, the Christian acceptance of a share in the lot of a crucified Savior, the loving participation in the painful effects of the presence of sin—devotion to the Sacred Heart is eminently fitting for our age.[4] Further, every Communion, while it is a celebration, is a sharing in the paschal mystery, and we know how much attention St. John (and after him the Fathers of the Church) placed on blood and water coming from the pierced side of Christ (John 19:34)—the Church coming from the Heart of Christ, say the Fathers, as the first Eve had come from the side of the first Adam.

A far cry, this, from the various consecration prayers, hymns and other manifestations of piety toward the Sacred Heart, with their contorted, ultrabaroque, sentimentalized imagery, not to mention the still existing graphic representations done in the most repulsive and decadent styles. Instead of damaging this devotion, the liturgical, Scriptural and artistic developments of our time should help purify it from these verbal and visual deformations.[5]

Devotion to the Blessed Sacrament is also sometimes thought to be in opposition to the spirit of the liturgy. Surely, the Constitution says nothing explicitly about Benediction or visits to the Blessed Sacrament. Surprising as this is, it must not be made to prove too much. For one thing, the Constitution makes no claim to give a complete liturgical theology. Secondly, it does not undercut the teaching of *Mediator Dei,* though it does accentuate different facets of the liturgy. *Mediator,* it must be noted, dedicates nine paragraphs to the importance of devotion to the Blessed Sacrament (#129–37) and reiterates the Council of Trent's solemn commendation of the practice (Session 13, canons 5 and 6).

Nevertheless, it is hard to escape the impression that, just as emphases have changed in the devotional life of the Church throughout the centuries, so they are changing today. The Appendix to the Constitution on the Liturgy describes the altar as "the place of the Eucharistic sacrifice and the venerable table for the sacred banquet" (#3). This is evidently quite a different liturgical vision from that of the baroque period, which treated the altar as principally a place of splendor for the divine presence, and still more distinct from that of the later Middle Ages, with intricate retables and reredoses. Yet the same Appendix suggests a preference for "a special chapel of the Eucharist rather extensively decorated," as "more fitting" for the veneration and worship of this great Sacrament (#6). Thus, while the emphasis shifts, the devotion remains.

The feast of Corpus Christi is, of course, the liturgical expression of the several meanings and uses of the Blessed Sacrament, a sort of Holy Thursday "seen from within," as Father Riepe suggests. While some of the ceremonies and processions connected with it are the outgrowth of the spiritual needs of the seven hundred years during which it has been celebrated, there is little doubt that today's mentality is less inclined toward some of these forms. Part of the change is, doubtless, a reaction against too one-sided a stress, as though the Blessed Sacrament were given us principally as an object to be worshiped.

Present-day theologians, accordingly, prefer to stress that "the real presence is not primarily something static," [6] as Father Charles Davis words it. He goes on to explain that "the primary expression of our belief in the real presence is the eating of the host, or communion. The symbolic activity here is eating. It is precisely because there is something which looks like bread and serves to symbolize and convey Christ that the Eucharist is a sacrament." And while there surely is room in our Eucharistic piety for what Romano Guardini calls "the sacred gaze," I find it hard to believe, as I mentioned earlier, that our Lord would have chosen precisely the symbol of bread if He intended the Eucharist principally as something to be adored.

It is common knowledge that originally the Blessed Sacrament was reserved principally in order to be available for Communion of the sick who could not be present at the Holy Sacrifice. Father Rahner has suggested that we can give our visits to the Blessed Sacrament a sound theological and liturgical orientation if we recall the full meaning of the Eucharist. The object of our devotions is the person of

Christ present in the sacrament as the food and life of our souls, the sacramental sign of the death-offering of Christ for our salvation. Thus it becomes the extension of our participation in the Mass and an anticipation of our next Holy Communion. Further, since the Eucharist is, in the Constitution's pregnant words, "a sign of unity, a bond of charity" (Article 47), such liturgically centered visits and devotion need not lead to exaggerated individualism or solipsistic piety; rather the contrary.[7]

It is certainly to be hoped that the ceremonies surrounding Benediction of the Blessed Sacrament will be changed to allow for more variety, more Scriptural and other liturgical enrichment. The presently prescribed prayers are too limited and specialized to serve a wide purpose. The *Tantum Ergo,* for example, while a magnificent and lapidary ending to the massive theological hymn *Pange Lingua,* is hardly an ideal hymn for every Benediction, particularly as it presupposes the rest of the *Pange Lingua* to make full sense (*ergo* means "therefore," and can hardly fit as a beginning). It was, like certain other familiar liturgical texts, tolerable as long as people sang it in Latin, not fully understanding it; but, in translation it now seems inadequate as well as monotonous.

The matter of thanksgiving after Mass has come up for some discussion, and even not a little distress, in the light of recent liturgical developments. *Mediator Dei* gave six paragraphs (123–28) to its importance. Yet the present brevity of the part of the Mass following Communion (now that the Prologue of St. John's Gospel and the Leonine prayers have been dropped) makes us more aware than ever that something needs to be done at this point. Perhaps a prescribed period of silence just before the Postcommunion prayer—one lasting several minutes, and not a few token

166

moments—could be of help. In this, I believe, the experience of the Quakers could be useful to us in stressing the importance of silence, not in isolation but in community, and precisely following our special instant of communion with Christ and each other. If any part of the Mass could be fruitfully lengthened, it would seem to be this.

I should also suggest that we take a hint from the Anglican practice of singing the Gloria at this point, rather than just before the Collect. A strong case, I believe, could be made for this change on both historical and liturgico-theological grounds. The Gloria is a magnificent paean of praise and thanksgiving, largely Christocentric in its thrust, and admirably suited to the need for community thanksgiving at the end of Mass, rather than to that of rallying the people toward the beginning. In its present location, it seems to put the "office of readings out of focus" and to "dilute the fundamental importance of the proclamation," as Nocent feels.[8] (I do not mean to suggest that Nocent, or Jungmann, who also treats the problem, advocates the change just suggested, or that all Anglicans follow the practice—a recent survey shows, in fact, that only 62 per cent do.)

Yet there is a deep need for thanksgiving in a more personal sense. Pope Paul recently spoke of the true Christian life requiring "silence, meditation, interior life and a mystic sense." [9] The very authenticity that all Christians aspire to presupposes interiority and at least some contemplation. As Father Paul Gramont says so well in "Liturgy and Contemplation," if we are not careful, "rites can become a facile means of evading religious reality and of preventing its striking deep into our hearts." [10] And one of the leading religious writers of our time, Father Hans Urs von Balthasar, in his treatise on *Prayer* (pages 97–98), shows how imperative contemplation is for liturgy. Without it, he believes, "the impression wrought by the liturgy grows faint in the course of daily life." And he adds: "A liturgical movement unaccompanied by a contemplative movement is a kind of romanticism, an escape." This is not to say that such contemplation should begin immediately after Mass; yet it is hard to think of a time when it is more appropriate.

Regarding thanksgiving after Mass, I hope that anyone who reads these pages will read Father Rahner's illuminating chapter, "Developing Eucharistic Devotion," in *The Christian Commitment*. While thanksgiving is not "binding under pain of sin," it is not superfluous. For one thing, the Roman liturgy, even revised, possesses a "certain aridity," indeed "a juridical austerity and a tendency to legalistic brevity, setting limits and barriers, psychologically and in terms of time." The Eastern liturgies are far more meditative, and in a good sense more subjective and emotional. We need a certain amount of time to achieve the "full, personal participation of spiritual, responsible persons." Further, we need an "intermediate zone between the liturgy and life in all its harsh reality, where the two meet: a zone in which the individual strives, in personal prayer, to immerse the spirit of the heavenly sacrifice in the corporeal stuff of earthly reality." This is not primarily a matter of thanksgiving, but of a "personal participation in the saving reality made present in the Mass."

This is the moment, it seems to me, for those who have been involved for years in struggling for the reform of the liturgy to redirect a portion of our energy into patient, conciliatory channels. I do not at all imply that we may rest on our laurels. The further changes that certainly lie ahead will need sympathy and understanding and interior acceptance, not external conformity, if they are to do the pastoral good for which they are intended. Otherwise they may become as extrinsic to prayer and sterile as some of the less meaningful ceremonies they replace.

In an age of ecumenical endeavor, surely there is place for what we may call "intramural ecumenism." "Dialogue is not restricted to contact with atheists, and pastoral concern does not justify pushing people around" is the wise advice of a far from reactionary group, the editors of *Cahiers d'Action Religieuse et Sociale* on pages 130–31 of the February 15, 1965, issue. Any note of triumph should be as out of place among liturgical progressives as it is odious when practiced by obstructionists or self-styled "traditionalists." If we look upon the Council's work as a sort of vindication— at least a partial one—of positions we have been laboring for, Christian charity and our own principles prevent us from treating it as a personal victory over anyone.

At the same time, there is little room for either self-congratulation or complacency. Inertia is always a threat, and sloth a sin that is not only deadly but also besetting. Pope Paul has repeatedly begged us not to return to the "quiet, devout and lazy practices of the past." The participation to which the Church summons us is, obviously, far from easy. It involves the effort of changing our church etiquette, working where once we could be passive, listening seriously instead of indulging in private thoughts or petitions. But it involves ever so much more: an interior posture of openness to the full demands of God's Word, an identification with Christ and His brothers in response to the encounter of the sacraments, a willingness to be His witnesses to the whole world.

There lurks yet another peril to which we may be susceptible even when we accept the centrality of the liturgy: that of feeling a sense of security once we have developed

169

our social participation in worship. For it is easier, most of us find, to pray with certain people than to work with them, easier to support a mission than to share in one.

Important as it is to build up a sense of community in worship, it is no less important to make sure that community does not degenerate into coterie. True, by Baptism and Confirmation we are initiated, and by Communion we share more deeply in Christ and the Mystical Christ. But the sending or mission implied in the *Ite missa est* (however it is translated) must not stop at the church door, or even in work for the conversion of our environment. Ours must not be a ghetto mission.

It has often been charged against the liturgical movement that one country in which it seemed most vital in the 1930s was the very country in which socialism took its most sinister form, Nazi Germany. During World War II, I occasionally did chaplain work in German prison camps and was much impressed by the earnestness of the German prisoners in liturgical participation. They sang like no congregation I had ever heard. Perhaps my information did not extend far enough, but it seemed that their solidarity stopped with the group or at least with the nation. True, the soldiers that came to Mass were not Nazis; indeed, it cost them more than a little, even in a prison camp, to attend Mass at all. But I could not help feeling that their social sense was less developed toward the whole world than toward the nation-group.

In a deeply disturbing and explosive essay on liturgical reform, contained in his controversial book *Honest to God*, the Anglican Bishop John A. T. Robinson points up a most surreptitious danger to which enthusiasm for liturgy may lead: that of "simply creating 'another world' of its own, a world where everything is 'done' according to the latest (or

170

the oldest) models and which yet merely goes on side by side with real life." He goes on to quote Eric James (*The Roots of the Liturgy,* page 5): "These actions will have an independent life of their own, an ecclesiastical life; something which belongs to the Church for its own sake; something which is neither natural nor necessarily supernatural." And he concludes: "The great danger is that liturgy creates a world of things over against the secular, instead of a vision of the sacredness of the secular."

This is not to say, of course, that the secular is the final aim of worship, as though man were elevated to the place of God. Rather, as I see it, it is that we must beware of making an idol of our own techniques, our own processes, falling into a subtler form of egoism, using God as a tool for securing self-satisfaction. Holy Scripture cautions us against pretending to love God, Whom we do not see, while we fail to love our neighbor, whom we do see. And we can never reflect too much on our Lord's criterion for judgment: "As often as you did it to one of these My least brethren, you did it to Me."

As this is being written we do not yet know the final contents of Schema XIII of Vatican Council II (on the Church in the contemporary world). However, after reading preliminary drafts of the Schema, and discussing it with several experts involved in its final presentation, I believe that the Christian's social responsibility to the world will be urgently pressed. Both the opening statement of the Council and the Constitution on the Church already indicate this as part of the laity's special vocation. Article 31 stresses that laymen have the vocation to "seek the kingdom of God by engaging in temporal affairs and by ordering them according to God's plan." The Christian laity are further to "learn the deepest meaning and the value of all creation, so that

171

the world may be permeated by the spirit of Christ and may more effectively fulfill its purpose in justice, charity and peace, remedying the customs and conditions of the world, and by so doing imbue culture and human activity with genuine moral values" (Article 36). An immense task, indeed, and one which opens up endless perspectives.

Thus, there can be nothing facile or prefabricated about the Christian's mission. Nor have we the right to suppose that a minimal liturgical attitude, or a merely literal compliance with the prescriptions of the Constitutions, will create the type of new Christian envisioned by the Council. Perhaps we can take a hint from the varied translations of *Ite missa est* that have been proposed. One, given more than twenty years ago by Father Gerald Ellard, was: "Go, you are commissioned!" Another is: "Go, fulfill your commitment!" Yet another: "Go, and do Christ's work!" In any case, we may take it as more than accident that the words Mass, mission, commission and commitment all have the same root meaning.

In one of the great religious documents of our wondrously productive age, Cardinal Cushing stressed that "a lack of social consciousness, a failure to be concerned for the welfare of our brothers" is a supreme scandal of Christian existence. On the other hand, "the liturgy, properly carried out, leads us to a consciousness of our brothers, for it is with them that we worship the Father." He insists that the renewed liturgy should help us get rid of that spirit of "rugged individualism," in the name of which so often we Catholics "excuse ourselves when we have been requested to become involved in the community."

It would be hard to find a clearer enunciation of this danger than these prophetic words of the Cardinal: "Liturgy which does not move its participants to social action is mere

172

ceremonialism; social action which does not find its source in the liturgy is mere humanitarianism." [11] For us Christians to become no more than humanitarians is a betrayal of Christ; for us to be less than humanitarian is an even more heinous betrayal.

Pope Paul put it much the same way, when he insisted that bearing the name of Christian—which is to say, of Christ —we are "doubly obliged to make the most characteristic contribution of the Christian to social life, a spontaneous, generous and persevering contribution by which the public can judge if our religious practice is sincere or hypocritical, and if the title of Christian is one of honor or of condemnation."

Rooted in the Incarnation, with all the built-in tensions and polarities implied in that great mystery, Christianity must ever work to achieve the dynamic poise between -isms, with their impulse to become exclusivisms. There have always been those Christians, distrustful or timid by nature, who have wanted to reduce the human element of the Incarnation and its prolongation in the Mystical Christ—the docetists, acosmists and other antihumanists. At the other pole are the extreme naturalists, the Pelagians of all shades, the secular humanists, who would reduce Christianity to mere anthropocentrism. [12]

The liturgy, understood in its broad, rich implications, offers the lines of solution, and to the extent that this is possible, at least the direction of a dynamic reconciliation of these tensions. As the worship of God, it remains sternly God-centered; as worship by God's people, it is no less strictly man-related. Each of us must judge for himself whether he is prone to one excess or the other. He can then also judge how best to use the liturgy as a corrective.

I should like to close this book with two quotations which

173

I believe illustrate the two-pronged responsibility of the liturgical Christian. They are both from a devout priest who worked hard throughout his life at resolving the tensions of the authentic Christian humanist. In *Le Christique,* written not long before he died, Father Teilhard de Chardin put his finger on the weakness of mere humanism: "These neo-humanisms of the twentieth century dehumanize us under too low a heaven." But he also warned Christians: "A religion judged to be inferior to our human ideal is a lost religion." [13]

APPENDIX ONE

Constitution on the Sacred Liturgy

Promulgated by
Pope Paul VI
at the closing of the
Second Session
of the
Second Vatican Council
December 4, 1963

INTRODUCTION

1. 𝒯his sacred Council has several aims in view: it desires to impart an ever increasing vigor to the Christian life of the faithful; to adapt more suitably to the needs of our own times those institutions which are subject to change; to foster whatever can promote union among all who believe in Christ; to strengthen whatever can help to call the whole of mankind into the household of the Church. The Council therefore sees particularly cogent reasons for undertaking the reform and promotion of the liturgy.

2. For the liturgy, "through which the work of our redemption is accomplished," [1]* most of all in the divine sacrifice of the Eucharist, is the outstanding means whereby the faithful may express in their lives, and manifest to others, the mystery of Christ and the real nature of the true Church. It is of the essence of the Church that she be both human and divine, visible and yet invisibly equipped, eager to act and yet intent on contemplation, present in this world and yet not at home in it; and she is all these things in such wise that in her the human is directed and subordinated to the divine, the visible likewise to the invisible, action to contemplation, and this present world to that city yet to come, which we seek.[2] While the liturgy daily builds up those who are within into a holy temple of the Lord, into a dwelling place for God in the Spirit,[3] to the mature measure of the fulness of Christ,[4] at the same time it marvelously strengthens their power to preach Christ, and thus shows forth the Church to those who are outside as a sign lifted

* *Notes* on the Constitution will be found on pp. 224–25.

176

up among the nations [5] under which the scattered children of God may be gathered together,[6] until there is one sheepfold and one shepherd.[7]

3. Wherefore the sacred Council judges that the following principles concerning the promotion and reform of the liturgy should be called to mind, and that practical norms should be established.

Among these principles and norms there are some which can and should be applied both to the Roman rite and also to all the other rites. The practical norms which follow, however, should be taken as applying only to the Roman rite, except for those which, in the very nature of things, affect other rites as well.

4. Lastly, in faithful obedience to tradition, the sacred Council declares that holy Mother Church holds all lawfully acknowledged rites to be of equal right and dignity; that she wishes to preserve them in the future and to foster them in every way. The Council also desires that, where necessary, the rites be revised carefully in the light of sound tradition, and that they be given new vigor to meet the circumstances and needs of modern times.

General Principles for the Restoration and Promotion of the Sacred Liturgy

I. *The Nature of the Sacred Liturgy and Its Importance in the Church's Life*

5. *G*od who "wills that all men be saved and come to the knowledge of the truth" (1 *Tim.* 2:4), "who in many and various ways spoke in times past to the fathers by the prophets" (*Heb.* 1:1), when the fulness of time had come sent His Son, the Word made flesh, anointed by the Holy Spirit, to preach the gospel to the poor, to heal the contrite of heart,[8] to be a "bodily and spiritual medicine," [9] the Mediator between God and man.[10] For His humanity, united with the person of the Word, was the instrument of our salvation. Therefore in Christ "the perfect achievement of our reconciliation came forth, and the fulness of divine worship was given to us." [11]

The wonderful works of God among the people of the Old Testament were but a prelude to the work of Christ the Lord in redeeming mankind and giving perfect glory to God. He

178

achieved His task principally by the paschal mystery of His blessed passion, resurrection from the dead, and glorious ascension, whereby "dying, he destroyed our death and, rising, he restored our life." [12] For it was from the side of Christ as He slept the sleep of death upon the cross that there came forth "the wondrous sacrament of the whole Church." [13]

6. Just as Christ was sent by the Father, so also He sent the apostles, filled with the Holy Spirit. This He did that, by preaching the gospel to every creature,[14] they might proclaim that the Son of God, by His death and resurrection, had freed us from the power of Satan [15] and from death, and brought us into the kingdom of His Father. His purpose also was that they might accomplish the work of salvation which they had proclaimed, by means of sacrifice and sacraments, around which the entire liturgical life revolves. Thus by baptism men are plunged into the paschal mystery of Christ: they die with Him, are buried with Him, and rise with Him; [16] they receive the spirit of adoption as sons "in which we cry: Abba, Father" (Rom. 8:15), and thus become true adorers whom the Father seeks.[17] In like manner, as often as they eat the supper of the Lord they proclaim the death of the Lord until He comes.[18] For that reason, on the very day of Pentecost, when the Church appeared before the world, "those who received the word" of Peter "were baptized." And "they continued steadfastly in the teaching of the apostles and in the communion of the breaking of bread and in prayers . . . praising God and being in favor with all the people" (Acts 2:41-47). From that time onwards the Church has never failed to come together to celebrate the paschal mystery: reading those things "which were in all the scriptures concerning him" (Luke 24:27), celebrating the Eucharist in which "the victory and triumph of his death are again made present," [19] and at the same time giving thanks "to

179

God for his unspeakable gift" (2 *Cor.* 9:15) in Christ Jesus, "in praise of his glory" (*Eph.* 1:12), through the power of the Holy Spirit.

7. To accomplish so great a work, Christ is always present in His Church, especially in her liturgical celebrations. He is present in the sacrifice of the Mass, not only in the person of His minister, "the same now offering, through the mystery of priests, who formerly offered himself on the cross," [20] but especially under the Eucharistic species. By His power He is present in the sacraments, so that when a man baptizes it is really Christ Himself who baptizes.[21] He is present in His word, since it is He Himself who speaks when the holy scriptures are read in the Church. He is present, lastly, when the Church prays and sings, for He promised: "Where two or three are gathered together in my name, there am I in the midst of them" (*Matt.* 18:20).

Christ indeed always associates the Church with Himself in this great work wherein God is perfectly glorified and men are sanctified. The Church is His beloved Bride who calls to her Lord, and through Him offers worship to the Eternal Father.

Rightly, then, the liturgy is considered as an exercise of the priestly office of Jesus Christ. In the liturgy the sanctification of man is signified by signs perceptible to the senses, and is effected in a way which corresponds with each of these signs; in the liturgy the whole public worship is performed by the Mystical Body of Jesus Christ, that is, by the Head and His members.

From this it follows that every liturgical celebration, because it is an action of Christ the priest and of His Body which is the Church, is a sacred action surpassing all others; no other action of the Church can equal its efficacy by the same title and to the same degree.

8. In the earthly liturgy we take part in a foretaste of that heavenly liturgy which is celebrated in the holy city of Jerusalem toward which we journey as pilgrims, where Christ is sitting at the right hand of God, a minister of the holies and of the true tabernacle; [22] we sing a hymn to the Lord's glory with all the warriors of the heavenly army; venerating the memory of the saints, we hope for some part and fellowship with them; we eagerly await the Savior, our Lord Jesus Christ, until He, our life, shall appear and we too will appear with Him in glory.[23]

9. The sacred liturgy does not exhaust the entire activity of the Church. Before men can come to the liturgy they must be called to faith and to conversion: "How then are they to call upon him in whom they have not yet believed? But how are they to believe him whom they have not heard? And how are they to hear if no one preaches? And how are men to preach unless they be sent?" (*Rom.* 10:14-15).

Therefore the Church announces the good tidings of salvation to those who do not believe, so that all men may know the true God and Jesus Christ whom He has sent, and may be converted from their ways, doing penance.[24] To believers also the Church must ever preach faith and penance; she must prepare them for the sacraments, teach them to observe all that Christ has commanded,[25] and invite them to all the works of charity, piety, and the apostolate. For all these works make it clear that Christ's faithful, though not of this world, are to be the light of the world and to glorify the Father before men.

10. Nevertheless the liturgy is the summit toward which the activity of the Church is directed; at the same time it is the fount from which all her power flows. For the aim and object of apostolic works is that all who are made sons of God by faith and baptism should come together to praise

181

God in the midst of His Church, to take part in the sacrifice, and to eat the Lord's supper.

The liturgy in its turn moves the faithful, filled with "the paschal sacraments," to be "one in holiness"; [26] it prays that "they may hold fast in their lives to what they have grasped by their faith"; [27] the renewal in the Eucharist of the covenant between the Lord and man draws the faithful into the compelling love of Christ and sets them on fire. From the liturgy, therefore, and especially from the Eucharist, as from a fount, grace is poured forth upon us; and the sanctification of men in Christ and the glorification of God, to which all other activities of the Church are directed as toward their end, is achieved in the most efficacious possible way.

11. But in order that the liturgy may be able to produce its full effects, it is necessary that the faithful come to it with proper dispositions, that their minds should be attuned to their voices, and that they should cooperate with divine grace lest they receive it in vain.[28] Pastors of souls must therefore realize that, when the liturgy is celebrated, something more is required than the mere observation of the laws governing valid and licit celebration; it is their duty also to ensure that the faithful take part fully aware of what they are doing, actively engaged in the rite, and enriched by its effects.

12. The spiritual life, however, is not limited solely to participation in the liturgy. The Christian is indeed called to pray with his brethren, but he must also enter into his chamber to pray to the Father in secret; [29] yet more, according to the teaching of the Apostle, he should pray without ceasing.[30] We learn from the same Apostle that we must always bear about in our body the dying of Jesus, so that the life also of Jesus may be made manifest in our bodily frame.[31] This is why we ask the Lord in the sacrifice of the Mass that, "receiving the offering of the spiritual victim," he may fashion us for himself "as an eternal gift." [32]

13. Popular devotions of the Christian people are to be highly commended, provided they accord with the laws and norms of the Church, above all when they are ordered by the Apostolic See.

Devotions proper to individual Churches also have a special dignity if they are undertaken by mandate of the bishops according to customs or books lawfully approved.

But these devotions should be so drawn up that they harmonize with the liturgical seasons, accord with the sacred liturgy, are in some fashion derived from it, and lead the people to it, since, in fact, the liturgy by its very nature far surpasses any of them.

II. *The Promotion of Liturgical Instruction and Active Participation*

14. Mother Church earnestly desires that all the faithful should be led to that full, conscious, and active participation in liturgical celebrations which is demanded by the very nature of the liturgy. Such participation by the Christian people as "a chosen race, a royal priesthood, a holy nation, a redeemed people" (I *Pet.* 2:9; cf. 2:4-5), is their right and duty by reason of their baptism.

In the restoration and promotion of the sacred liturgy, this full and active participation by all the people is the aim to be considered before all else; for it is the primary and indispensable source from which the faithful are to derive the true Christian spirit; and therefore pastors of souls must zealously strive to achieve it, by means of the necessary instruction, in all their pastoral work.

Yet it would be futile to entertain any hopes of realizing this unless the pastors themselves, in the first place, become thoroughly imbued with the spirit and power of the liturgy, and undertake to give instruction about it. A prime need, therefore, is that attention be directed, first of all, to the liturgical instruction of the clergy. Wherefore the sacred Council has decided to enact as follows:

15. Professors who are appointed to teach liturgy in seminaries, religious houses of study, and theological faculties must be properly trained for their work in institutes which specialize in this subject.

16. The study of sacred liturgy is to be ranked among the compulsory and major courses in seminaries and religious houses of studies; in theological faculties it is to rank among the principal courses. It is to be taught under its theological, historical, spiritual, pastoral, and juridical aspects. Moreover, other professors, while striving to expound the mystery of Christ and the history of salvation from the angle proper to each of their own subjects, must nevertheless do so in a way which will clearly bring out the connection between their subjects and the liturgy, as also the unity which underlies all priestly training. This consideration is especially important for professors of dogmatic, spiritual, and pastoral theology and for those of holy scripture.

17. In seminaries and houses of religious, clerics shall be given a liturgical formation in their spiritual life. For this they will need proper direction, so that they may be able to understand the sacred rites and take part in them wholeheartedly; and they will also need personally to celebrate the sacred mysteries, as well as popular devotions which are imbued with the spirit of the liturgy. In addition they must learn how to observe the liturgical laws, so that life in seminaries and houses of religion may be thoroughly influenced by the spirit of the liturgy.

18. Priests, both secular and religious, who are already working in the Lord's vineyard are to be helped by every suitable means to understand ever more fully what it is that they are doing when they perform sacred rites; they are to

184

be aided to live the liturgical life and to share it with the faithful entrusted to their care.

19. With zeal and patience, pastors of souls must promote the liturgical instruction of the faithful, and also their active participation in the liturgy both internally and externally, taking into account their age and condition, their way of life, and standard of religious culture. By so doing, pastors will be fulfilling one of the chief duties of a faithful dispenser of the mysteries of God; and in this matter they must lead their flock not only in word but also by example.

20. Transmissions of the sacred rites by radio and television shall be done with discretion and dignity, under the leadership and direction of a suitable person appointed for this office by the bishops. This is especially important when the service to be broadcast is the Mass.

III. *The Reform of the Sacred Liturgy*

21. In order that the Christian people may more certainly derive an abundance of graces from the sacred liturgy, holy Mother Church desires to undertake with great care a general restoration of the liturgy itself. For the liturgy is made up of immutable elements divinely instituted, and of elements subject to change. These not only may but ought to be changed with the passage of time if they have suffered from the intrusion of anything out of harmony with the inner nature of the liturgy or have become unsuited to it.

In this restoration, both texts and rites should be drawn up so that they express more clearly the holy things which they signify; the Christian people, so far as possible, should be enabled to understand them with ease and to take part in them fully, actively, and as befits a community.

Wherefore the sacred Council establishes the following general norms:

(A) *General Norms*

22. §1. Regulation of the sacred liturgy depends solely on the authority of the Church, that is, on the Apostolic See and, as laws may determine, on the bishop.

§2. In virtue of power conceded by the law, the regulation of the liturgy within certain defined limits belongs also to various kinds of competent territorial bodies of bishops legitimately established.

§3. Therefore no other person, even if he be a priest, may add, remove, or change anything in the liturgy on his own authority.

23. That sound tradition may be retained, and yet the way remain open to legitimate progress, a careful investigation is always to be made into each part of the liturgy which is to be revised. This investigation should be theological, historical, and pastoral. Also the general laws governing the structure and meaning of the liturgy must be studied in conjunction with the experience derived from recent liturgical reforms and from the indults conceded to various places. Finally, there must be no innovations unless the good of the Church genuinely and certainly requires them; and care must be taken that any new forms adopted should in some way grow organically from forms already existing.

As far as possible, notable differences between the rites used in adjacent regions must be carefully avoided.

24. Sacred scripture is of the greatest importance in the celebration of the liturgy. For it is from scripture that lessons are read and explained in the homily, and psalms are sung; the prayers, collects, and liturgical songs are scriptural in their inspiration, and it is from the scriptures that actions and signs derive their meaning. Thus to achieve the restoration, progress, and adaptation of the sacred liturgy, it is

essential to promote that warm and living love for scripture to which the venerable tradition of both eastern and western rites gives testimony.

25. The liturgical books are to be revised as soon as possible; experts are to be employed on the task, and bishops are to be consulted, from various parts of the world.

(B) *Norms Drawn from the Hierarchic and Communal Nature of the Liturgy*

26. Liturgical services are not private functions, but are celebrations of the Church, which is the "sacrament of unity," namely, the holy people united and ordered under their bishops.[33]

Therefore liturgical services pertain to the whole body of the Church; they manifest it and have effects upon it; but they concern the individual members of the Church in different ways, according to their differing rank, office, and actual participation.

27. It is to be stressed that whenever rites, according to their specific nature, make provision for communal celebration involving the presence and active participation of the faithful, this way of celebrating them is to be preferred, so far as possible, to a celebration that is individual and quasi-private.

This applies with especial force to the celebration of Mass and the administration of the sacraments, even though every Mass has of itself a public and social nature.

28. In liturgical celebrations, each person, minister or layman, who has an office to perform, should do all of, but only, those parts which pertain to his office by the nature of the rite and the principles of liturgy.

29. Servers, lectors, commentators, and members of the choir also exercise a genuine liturgical function. They ought,

therefore, to discharge their office with the sincere piety and decorum demanded by so exalted a ministry and rightly expected of them by God's people.

Consequently they must all be deeply imbued with the spirit of the liturgy, each in his own measure, and they must be trained to perform their functions in a correct and orderly manner.

30. To promote active participation, the people should be encouraged to take part by means of acclamations, responses, psalmody, antiphons, and songs, as well as by actions, gestures, and bodily attitudes. And at the proper times all should observe a reverent silence.

31. The revision of the liturgical books must carefully attend to the provision of rubrics also for the people's parts.

32. The liturgy makes distinctions between persons according to their liturgical function and sacred Orders, and there are liturgical laws providing for due honors to be given to civil authorities. Apart from these instances, no special honors are to be paid in the liturgy to any private persons or classes of persons, whether in the ceremonies or by external display.

(C) *Norms Based upon the Didactic and Pastoral Nature of the Liturgy*

33. Although the sacred liturgy is above all things the worship of the divine Majesty, it likewise contains much instruction for the faithful.[34] For in the liturgy God speaks to His people and Christ is still proclaiming His gospel. And the people reply to God both by song and prayer.

Moreover, the prayers addressed to God by the priest who presides over the assembly in the person of Christ are said in the name of the entire holy people and of all present. And the visible signs used by the liturgy to signify invisible divine things have been chosen by Christ or the Church. Thus not only when things are read "which were written for our instruction" (*Rom.* 15:4), but also when the Church prays or sings or acts, the faith of those taking part is nourished and their minds are raised to God, so that they may offer Him their rational service and more abundantly receive His grace.

Wherefore, in the revision of the liturgy, the following general norms should be observed:

34. The rites should be distinguished by a noble simplicity; they should be short, clear, and unencumbered by useless repetitions; they should be within the people's powers of comprehension, and normally should not require much explanation.

35. That the intimate connection between words and rites may be apparent in the liturgy:

(1) In sacred celebrations there is to be more reading from holy scripture, and it is to be more varied and suitable.

(2) Because the sermon is part of the liturgical service, the best place for it is to be indicated even in the rubrics, as far as the nature of the rite will allow; the ministry of preaching is to be fulfilled with exactitude and fidelity. The sermon, moreover, should draw its content mainly from scriptural and liturgical sources, and its character should be that of a proclamation of God's wonderful works in the history of salvation, the mystery of Christ, ever made present and active within us, especially in the celebration of the liturgy.

(3) Instruction which is more explicitly liturgical should also be given in a variety of ways; if necessary, short directives to be spoken by the priest or proper minister should be provided within the rites themselves. But they should occur only at the more suitable moments, and be in prescribed or similar words.

(4) Bible services should be encouraged, especially on the vigils of the more solemn feasts, on some weekdays in

Advent and Lent, and on Sundays and feast days. They are particularly to be commended in places where no priest is available; when this is so a deacon or some other person authorized by the bishop should preside over the celebration.

36. §1. Particular law remaining in force, the use of the Latin language is to be preserved in the Latin rites.

§2. But since the use of the mother tongue, whether in the Mass, the administration of the sacraments, or other parts of the liturgy, frequently may be of great advantage to the people, the limits of its employment may be extended. This will apply in the first place to the readings and directives, and to some of the prayers and chants, according to the regulations on this matter to be laid down separately in subsequent chapters.

§3. These norms being observed, it is for the competent territorial ecclesiastical authority mentioned in Art. 22, §2, to decide whether, and to what extent, the vernacular language is to be used; their decrees are to be approved, that is, confirmed, by the Apostolic See. And, whenever it seems to be called for, this authority is to consult with bishops of neighboring regions which have the same language.

§4. Translations from the Latin text into the mother tongue intended for use in the liturgy must be approved by the competent territorial ecclesiastical authority mentioned above.

(D) Norms for Adapting the Liturgy to the Culture and Traditions of Peoples

37. Even in the liturgy, the Church has no wish to impose a rigid uniformity in matters which do not implicate the faith or the good of the whole community; rather does she respect and foster the genius and talents of the various races and peoples. Anything in these peoples' way of life which is not indissolubly bound up with superstition and error she

studies with sympathy and, if possible, preserves intact. Sometimes in fact she admits such things into the liturgy itself, so long as they harmonize with its true and authentic spirit.

38. Provisions shall also be made, when revising the liturgical books, for legitimate variations and adaptations to different groups, regions, and peoples, especially in mission lands, provided that the substantial unity of the Roman rite is preserved; and this should be borne in mind when drawing up the rites and devising rubrics.

39. Within the limits set by the typical editions of the liturgical books, it shall be for the competent territorial ecclesiastical authority mentioned in Art. 22 §2, to specify adaptations, especially in the case of the administration of the sacraments, the sacramentals, processions, liturgical language, sacred music, and the arts, but according to the fundamental norms laid down in this Constitution.

40. In some places and circumstances, however, an even more radical adaptation of the liturgy is needed, and this entails greater difficulties.

Wherefore:

(1) The competent territorial ecclesiastical authority mentioned in Art. 22, §2, must, in this matter, carefully and prudently consider which elements from the traditions and culture of individual peoples might appropriately be admitted into divine worship. Adaptations which are judged to be useful or necessary should then be submitted to the Apostolic See, by whose consent they may be introduced.

(2) To ensure that adaptations may be made with all the circumspection which they demand, the Apostolic See will grant power to this same territorial ecclesiastical authority to permit and to direct, as the case requires, the necessary preliminary experiments over a determined period of time among certain groups suited for the purpose.

(3) Because liturgical laws often involve special difficulties with respect to adaptation, particularly in mission lands, men who are experts in these matters must be employed to formulate them.

IV. *Promotion of Liturgical Life in Diocese and Parish*

41. The bishop is to be considered as the high priest of his flock, from whom the life in Christ of his faithful is in some way derived and dependent.

Therefore all should hold in great esteem the liturgical life of the diocese centered around the bishop, especially in his cathedral church; they must be convinced that the preeminent manifestation of the Church consists in the full active participation of all God's holy people in these liturgical celebrations, especially in the same Eucharist, in a single prayer, at one altar, at which there presides the bishop surrounded by his college of priests and by his ministers.[35]

42. But because it is impossible for the bishop always and everywhere to preside over the whole flock in his Church, he cannot do other than establish lesser groupings of the faithful. Among these the parishes, set up locally under a pastor who takes the place of the bishop, are the most important: for in some manner they represent the visible Church constituted throughout the world.

And therefore the liturgical life of the parish and its relationship to the bishop must be fostered theoretically and practically among the faithful and clergy; efforts also must be made to encourage a sense of community within the parish, above all in the common celebration of the Sunday Mass.

V. *The Promotion of Pastoral-Liturgical Action*

43. Zeal for the promotion and restoration of the liturgy

is rightly held to be a sign of the providential dispositions of God in our time, as a movement of the Holy Spirit in His Church. It is today a distinguishing mark of the Church's life, indeed of the whole tenor of contemporary religious thought and action.

So that this pastoral-liturgical action may become even more vigorous in the Church, the sacred Council decrees:

44. It is desirable that the competent territorial ecclesiastical authority mentioned in Art. 22, §2, set up a liturgical commission, to be assisted by experts in liturgical science, sacred music, art, and pastoral practice. So far as possible the commission should be aided by some kind of Institute for Pastoral Liturgy, consisting of persons who are eminent in these matters, and including laymen as circumstances suggest. Under the direction of the above-mentioned territorial ecclesiastical authority the commission is to regulate pastoral-liturgical action throughout the territory, and to promote studies and necessary experiments whenever there is question of adaptations to be proposed to the Apostolic See.

45. For the same reason every diocese is to have a commission on the sacred liturgy under the direction of the bishop, for promoting the liturgical apostolate.

Sometimes it may be expedient that several dioceses should form between them one single commission which will be able to promote the liturgy by common consultation.

46. Besides the commission on the sacred liturgy, every diocese, as far as possible, should have commissions for sacred music and sacred art.

These three commissions must work in closest collaboration; indeed it will often be best to fuse the three of them into one single commission.

Chapter II

The Most Sacred Mystery of the Eucharist

47. *A*t the Last Supper, on the night when He was betrayed, our Savior instituted the Eucharistic sacrifice of His Body and Blood. He did this in order to perpetuate the sacrifice of the Cross throughout the centuries until He should come again, and so to entrust to His beloved spouse, the Church, a memorial of His death and resurrection: a sacrament of love, a sign of unity, a bond of charity,[36] a paschal banquet in which Christ is eaten, the mind is filled with grace, and a pledge of future glory is given to us.[37]

48. The Church, therefore, earnestly desires that Christ's faithful, when present at this mystery of faith, should not be there as strangers or silent spectators; on the contrary, through a good understanding of the rites and prayers they should take part in the sacred action conscious of what they are doing, with devotion and full collaboration. They should be instructed by God's word and be nourished at the table of the Lord's body; they should give thanks to God; by offering the Immaculate Victim, not only through the hands of the priest, but also with him, they should learn also to offer themselves; through Christ the Mediator,[38] they should be drawn

194

day by day into ever more perfect union with God and with each other, so that finally God may be all in all.

49. For this reason the sacred Council, having in mind those Masses which are celebrated with the assistance of the faithful, especially on Sundays and feasts of obligation, has made the following decrees in order that the sacrifice of the Mass, even in the ritual forms of its celebration, may become pastorally efficacious to the fullest degree.

50. The rite of the Mass is to be revised in such a way that the intrinsic nature and purpose of its several parts, as also the connection between them, may be more clearly manifested, and that devout and active participation by the faithful may be more easily achieved.

For this purpose the rites are to be simplified, due care being taken to preserve their substance; elements which, with the passage of time, came to be duplicated, or were added with but little advantage, are now to be discarded; other elements which have suffered injury through accidents of history are now to be restored to the vigor which they had in the days of the holy Fathers, as may seem useful or necessary.

51. The treasures of the bible are to be opened up more lavishly, so that richer fare may be provided for the faithful at the table of God's word. In this way a more representative portion of the holy scriptures will be read to the people in the course of a prescribed number of years.

52. By means of the homily the mysteries of the faith and the guiding principles of the Christian life are expounded from the sacred text, during the course of the liturgical year; the homily, therefore, is to be highly esteemed as part of the liturgy itself; in fact, at those Masses which are celebrated with the assistance of the people on Sundays and feasts of obligation, it should not be omitted except for a seroius reason.

53. Especially on Sundays and feasts of obligation there is to be restored, after the Gospel and the homily, "the common prayer" or "the prayer of the faithful." By this prayer, in which the people are to take part, intercession will be made for holy Church, for the civil authorities, for those oppressed by various needs, for all mankind, and for the salvation of the entire world.[39]

54. In Masses which are celebrated with the people, a suitable place may be allotted to their mother tongue. This is to apply in the first place to the readings and "the common prayer," but also, as local conditions may warrant, to those parts which pertain to the people, according to the norm laid down in Art. 36 of this Constitution.

Nevertheless steps should be taken so that the faithful may also be able to say or to sing together in Latin those parts of the Ordinary of the Mass which pertain to them.

And wherever a more extended use of the mother tongue within the Mass appears desirable, the regulation laid down in Art. 40 of this Constitution is to be observed.

55. That more perfect form of participation in the Mass whereby the faithful, after the priest's communion, receive the Lord's body from the same sacrifice, is strongly commended.

The dogmatic principles which were laid down by the Council of Trent remaining intact,[40] communion under both kinds may be granted when the bishops think fit, not only to clerics and religious, but also to the laity, in cases to be determined by the Apostolic See, as, for instance, to the newly ordained in the Mass of their sacred ordination, to the newly professed in the Mass of their religious profession, and to the newly baptized in the Mass which follows their baptism.

56. The two parts which, in a certain sense, go to make up the Mass, namely, the liturgy of the word and the Eucharistic

liturgy, are so closely connected with each other that they form but one single act of worship. Accordingly this sacred Synod strongly urges pastors of souls that, when instructing the faithful, they insistently teach them to take their part in the entire Mass, especially on Sundays and feasts of obligation.

57. §1. Concelebration, whereby the unity of the priesthood is appropriately manifested, has remained in use to this day in the Church both in the east and in the west. For this reason it has seemed good to the Council to extend permission for concelebration to the following cases:

1. (a) on the Thursday of the Lord's Supper, not only at the Mass of the Chrism, but also at the evening Mass;
    (b) at Masses during councils, bishops' conferences, and synods;
    (c) at the Mass for the blessing of an abbot.

2. Also, with permission of the ordinary, to whom it belongs to decide whether concelebration is opportune:
    (a) at conventual Mass, and at the principal Mass in churches when the needs of the faithful do not require that all the priests available should celebrate individually;
    (b) at Masses celebrated at any kind of priests' meetings, whether the priests be secular clergy or religious.

§2. 1. The regulation, however, of the discipline of concelebration in the diocese pertains to the bishop.
    2. Nevertheless, each priest shall always retain his right to celebrate Mass individually, though not

at the same time in the same church as a concelebrated Mass, nor on Thursday of the Lord's
Supper.

58. A new rite for concelebration is to be drawn up and
inserted into the Pontifical and into the Roman Missal.

Chapter III

The Other Sacraments and the Sacramentals

59.   The purpose of the sacraments is to sanctify men, to build up the body of Christ, and, finally, to give worship to God; because they are signs they also instruct. They not only presuppose faith, but by words and objects they also nourish, strengthen, and express it; that is why they are called "sacraments of faith." They do indeed impart grace, but, in addition, the very act of celebrating them most effectively disposes the faithful to receive this grace in a fruitful manner, to worship God duly, and to practice charity.

It is therefore of the highest importance that the faithful should easily understand the sacramental signs, and should frequent with great eagerness those sacraments which were instituted to nourish the Christian life.

60. Holy Mother Church has, moreover, instituted sacramentals. These are sacred signs which bear a resemblance to the sacraments: they signify effects, particularly of a spiritual kind, which are obtained through the Church's intercession. By them men are disposed to receive the chief effect of the sacraments, and various occasions in life are rendered holy.

61. Thus, for well-disposed members of the faithful, the

liturgy of the sacraments and sacramentals sanctifies almost every event in their lives; they are given access to the stream of divine grace which flows from the paschal mystery of the passion, death, and resurrection of Christ, the fount from which all sacraments and sacramentals draw their power. There is hardly any proper use of material things which cannot thus be directed toward the sanctification of men and the praise of God.

62. With the passage of time, however, there have crept into the rites of the sacraments and sacramentals certain features which have rendered their nature and purpose far from clear to the people of today; hence some changes have become necessary to adapt them to the needs of our own times. For this reason the sacred Council decrees as follows concerning their revision.

63. Because the use of the mother tongue in the administration of the sacraments and sacramentals can often be of considerable help to the people, this use is to be extended according to the following norms:

(a) The vernacular language may be used in administering the sacraments and sacramentals, according to the norm of Art. 36.

(b) In harmony with the new edition of the Roman Ritual, particular rituals shall be prepared without delay by the competent territorial ecclesiastical authority mentioned in Art. 22, §2, of this Constitution. These rituals, which are to be adapted, also as regards the language employed, to the needs of the different regions, are to be reviewed by the Apostolic See and then introduced into the regions for which they have been prepared. But in drawing up these rituals or particular collections of rites, the instructions prefixed to the individual rites in the Roman Ritual, whether they be pastoral and rubrical or whether they have special social import, shall not be omitted.

64. The catechumenate for adults, comprising several distinct steps, is to be restored and to be taken into use at the discretion of the local ordinary. By this means the time of the catechumenate, which is intended as a period of suitable instruction, may be sanctified by sacred rites to be celebrated at successive intervals of time.

65. In mission lands it is found that some of the peoples already make use of initiation rites. Elements from these, when capable of being adapted to Christian ritual, may be admitted along with those already found in Christian tradition, according to the norm laid down in Art. 37-40 of this Constitution.

66. Both of the rites for the baptism of adults are to be revised: not only the simpler rite, but also the more solemn one, which must take into account the restored catechumenate. A special Mass "for the conferring of baptism" is to be inserted into the Roman Missal.

67. The rite for the baptism of infants is to be revised, and it should be adapted to the circumstance that those to be baptized are, in fact, infants. The roles of parents and godparents, and also their duties, should be brought out more clearly in the rite itself.

68. The baptismal rite should contain variants, to be used at the discretion of the local ordinary, for occasions when a very large number are to be baptized together. Moreover, a shorter rite is to be drawn up, especially for mission lands, to be used by catechists, but also by the faithful in general when there is danger of death, and neither priest nor deacon is available.

69. In place of the rite called the "Order of supplying

what was omitted in the baptism of an infant," a new rite is to be drawn up. This should manifest more fittingly and clearly that the infant, baptized by the short rite, has already been received into the Church.

And a new rite is to be drawn up for converts who have already been validly baptized; it should indicate that they are now admitted to communion with the Church.

70. Except during Eastertide, baptismal water may be blessed within the rite of baptism itself by an approved shorter formula.

71. The rite of confirmation is to be revised and the intimate connection which this sacrament has with the whole of Christian initiation is to be more clearly set forth; for this reason it is fitting for candidates to renew their baptismal promises just before they are confirmed.

Confirmation may be given within the Mass when convenient; when it is given outside the Mass, the rite that is used should be introduced by a formula to be drawn up for this purpose.

72. The rite and formulas for the sacrament of penance are to be revised so that they more clearly express both the nature and effect of the sacrament.

73. "Extreme unction," which may also and more fittingly be called "anointing of the sick," is not a sacrament for those only who are at the point of death. Hence, as soon as any one of the faihtful begins to be in danger of death from sickness or old age, the fitting time for him to receive this sacrament has certainly already arrived.

74. In addition to the separate rites for anointing of the sick and for Viaticum, a continuous rite shall be prepared according to which the sick man is anointed after he has made his confession and before he receives Viaticum.

75. The number of the anointings is to be adapted to the

occasion, and the prayers which belong to the rite of anointing are to be revised so as to correspond with the varying conditions of the sick who receive the sacrament.

76. Both the ceremonies and texts of the ordination rites are to be revised. The address given by the bishop at the beginning of each ordination or consecration may be in the mother tongue.

When a bishop is consecrated, the laying of hands may be done by all the bishops present.

77. The marriage rite now found in the Roman Ritual is to be revised and enriched in such a way that the grace of the sacrament is more clearly signified and the duties of the spouses are taught.

"If any regions are wont to use other praiseworthy customs and ceremonies when celebrating the sacrament of matrimony, the sacred Synod earnestly desires that these by all means be retained".[41]

Moreover the competent territorial ecclesiastical authority mentioned in Art. 22, §2, of this Constitution is free to draw up its own rite suited to the usages of place and people, according to the provision of Art. 63. But the rite must always conform to the law that the priest assisting at the marriage must ask for and obtain the consent of the contracting parties.

78. Matrimony is normally to be celebrated within the Mass, after the reading of the gospel and the homily, and before "the prayer of the faithful." The prayer for the bride, duly amended to remind both spouses of their equal obligation to remain faithful to each other, may be said in the mother tongue.

But if the sacrament of matrimony is celebrated apart from Mass, the epistle and gospel from the nuptial Mass are to be read at the beginning of the rite, and the blessing should always be given to the spouses.

79. The sacramentals are to undergo a revision which takes into account the primary principle of enabling the faithful to participate intelligently, actively, and easily; the circumstances of our own days must also be considered. When rituals are revised, as laid down in Art. 63, new sacramentals may also be added as the need for these becomes apparent.

Reserved blessings shall be very few; reservations shall be in favor only of bishops or ordinaries.

Let provisions be made that some sacramentals, at least in special circumstances and at the discretion of the ordinary, may be administered by qualified lay persons.

80. The rite for the consecration of virgins at present found in the Roman Pontifical is to be revised.

Moreover, a rite of religious profession and renewal of vows shall be drawn up in order to achieve greater unity, sobriety, and dignity. Apart from exceptions in particular law, this rite should be adopted by those who make their profession or renewal of vows within the Mass.

Religious profession should preferably be made within the Mass.

81. The rite for the burial of the dead should express more clearly the paschal character of Christian death, and should correspond more closely to the circumstances and traditions found in various regions. This holds good also for the liturgical color to be used.

82. The rite for the burial of infants is to be revised, and a special Mass for the occasion should be provided.

Chapter IV

The Divine Office

83. *C*hrist Jesus, high priest of the new and eternal covenant, taking human nature, introduced into this earthly exile that hymn which is sung throughout all ages in the halls of heaven. He joins the entire community of mankind to Himself, associating it with His own singing of this canticle of divine praise.

For He continues His priestly work through the agency of His Church, which is ceaselessly engaged in praising the Lord and interceding for the salvation of the whole world. She does this, not only by celebrating the Eucharist, but also in other ways, especially by praying the divine office.

84. By tradition going back to early Christian times, the divine office is devised so that the whole course of the day and night is made holy by the praises of God. Therefore, when this wonderful song of praise is rightly performed by priests and others who are deputed for this purpose by the Church's ordinance, or by the faithful praying together with the priest in the approved form, then it is truly the voice of the bride addressed to her bridegroom; it is the very prayer which Christ Himself, together with His body, addresses to the Father.

85. Hence all who render this service are not only fulfilling a duty of the Church, but also are sharing in the greatest honor of Christ's spouse, for by offering these praises to God they are standing before God's throne in the name of the Church their Mother.

86. Priests who are engaged in the sacred pastoral ministry will offer the praises of the hours with greater fervor the more vividly they realize that they must heed St. Paul's exhortation: "Pray without ceasing" (1 *Thess.* 5:17). For the work in which they labor will effect nothing and bring forth no fruit except by the power of the Lord who said: "Without me you can do nothing" (*John* 15:5). That is why the apostles, instituting deacons, said: "We will devote ourselves to prayer and to the ministry of the word" (*Acts* 6:4).

87. In order that the divine office may be better and more perfectly prayed in existing circumstances, whether by priests or by other members of the Church, the sacred Council, carrying further the restoration already so happily begun by the Apostolic See, has seen fit to decree as follows concerning the office of the Roman rite.

88. Because the purpose of the office is to sanctify the day, the traditional sequence of the hours is to be restored so that once again they may be genuinely related to the time of the day when they are prayed, as far as this may be possible. Moreover, it will be necessary to take into account the modern conditions in which daily life has to be lived, especially by those who are called to labor in apostolic works.

89. Therefore, when the office is revised, these norms are to be observed:

(a) By the venerable tradition of the universal Church, Lauds as morning prayer and Vespers as evening prayer are the two hinges on which the daily office turns; hence they are to be considered as the chief hours and are to be celebrated as such.

(b) Compline is to be drawn up so that it will be a suitable prayer for the end of the day.

(c) The hour known as Matins, although it should retain the character of nocturnal praise when celebrated in choir, shall be adapted so that it may be recited at any hour of the day; it shall be made up of fewer psalms and longer readings.

(d) The hour of Prime is to be suppressed.

(e) In choir the minor hours of Terce, Sext, and None are to be observed. But outside choir it will be lawful to select any one of these three, according to the respective time of the day.

90. The divine office, because it is the public prayer of the Church, is a source of piety and nourishment for personal prayer. And therefore priests and all others who take part in the divine office are earnestly exhorted in the Lord to attune their minds to their voices when praying it. The better to achieve this, let them take steps to improve their understanding of the liturgy and of the bible, especially of the psalms.

In revising the Roman office, its ancient and venerable treasures are to be so adapted that all those to whom they are handed on may more extensively and easily draw profit from them.

91. So that it may really be possible in practice to observe the course of the hours proposed in Art. 89, the psalms are no longer to be distributed throughout one week, but through some longer period of time.

The work of revising the psalter, already happily begun, is to be finished as soon as possible, and is to take into account the style of Christian Latin, the liturgical use of psalms, also when sung, and the entire tradition of the Latin Church.

92. As regards the readings, the following shall be observed:

(a) Readings from sacred scripture shall be arranged so that the riches of God's word may be easily accessible in more abundant measure.

(b) Readings excerpted from the words of the fathers, doctors, and ecclesiastical writers shall be better selected.

(c) The accounts of martyrdom or the lives of the saints are to accord with the facts of history.

93. To whatever extent may seem desirable, the hymns are to be restored to their original form, and whatever smacks of mythology or ill accords with Christian piety is to be removed or changed. Also, as occasion may arise, let other selections from the treasury of hymns be incorporated.

94. That the day may be truly sanctified, and that the hours themselves may be recited with spiritual advantage, it is best that each of them be prayed at a time which most closely corresponds with its true canonical time.

95. Communities obliged to choral office are bound to celebrate the office in choir every day in addition to the conventual Mass. In particular:

(a) Orders of canons, of monks and of nuns, and of other regulars bound by law or constitutions to choral office must celebrate the entire office.

(b) Cathedral or collegiate chapters are bound to recite those parts of the office imposed on them by general or particular law.

(c) All members of the above communities who are in major orders or who are solemnly professed, except for lay brothers, are bound to recite individually those canonical hours which they do not pray in choir.

96. Clerics not bound to office in choir, if they are in major

orders, are bound to pray the entire office every day, either in common or individually, as laid down in Art. 89.

97. Appropriate instances are to be defined by the rubrics in which a liturgical service may be substituted for the divine office.

In particular cases, and for a just reason, ordinaries can dispense their subjects wholly or in part from the obligation of reciting the divine office, or may commute the obligation.

98. Members of any institute dedicated to acquiring perfection who, according to their constitutions, are to recite any parts of the divine office are thereby performing the public prayer of the Church.

They too perform the public prayer of the Church who, in virtue of their constitutions, recite any short office, provided this is drawn up after the pattern of the divine office and is duly approved.

99. Since the divine office is the voice of the Church, that is, of the whole mystical body publicly praising God, those clerics who are not obliged to office in choir, especially priests who live together or who assemble for any purpose, are urged to pray at least some part of the divine office in common.

All who pray the divine office, whether in choir or in common, should fulfil the task entrusted to them as perfectly as possible: this refers not only to the internal devotion of their minds but also to their external manner of celebration.

It is, moreover, fitting that the office, both in choir and in common, be sung when possible.

100. Pastors of souls should see to it that the chief hours, especially Vespers, are celebrated in common in church on Sundays and the more solemn feasts. And the laity, too, are encouraged to recite the divine office, either with the priests, or among themselves, or even individually.

101. §1. In accordance with the centuries-old tradition of

the Latin rite, the Latin language is to be retained by clerics in the divine office. But in individual cases the ordinary has the power of granting the use of a vernacular translation to those clerics for whom the use of Latin constitutes a grave obstacle to their praying the office properly. The vernacular version, however, must be one that is drawn up according to the provision of Art. 36.

§2. The competent superior has the power to grant the use of the vernacular in the celebration of the divine office, even in choir, to nuns and to members of institutes dedicated to acquiring perfection, both men who are not clerics and women. The version, however, must be one that is approved.

§3. Any cleric bound to the divine office fulfills his obligation if he prays the office in the vernacular together with a group of the faithful or with those mentioned in §2 above, provided that the text of the translation is approved.

Chapter V

The Liturgical Year

102. Holy Mother Church is conscious that she must celebrate the saving work of her divine Spouse by devoutly recalling it on certain days throughout the course of the year. Every week, on the day which she has called the Lord's day, she keeps the memory of the Lord's resurrection, which she also celebrates once in the year, together with His blessed passion, in the most solemn festival of Easter.

Within the cycle of a year, moreover, she unfolds the whole mystery of Christ, from the incarnation and birth until the ascension, the day of Pentecost, and the expectation of blessed hope and of the coming of the Lord.

Recalling thus the mysteries of redemption, the Church opens to the faithful the riches of her Lord's powers and merits, so that these are in some way made present for all time, and the faithful are enabled to lay hold upon them and become filled with saving grace.

103. In celebrating this annual cycle of Christ's mysteries, holy Church honors with especial love the Blessed Mary, Mother of God, who is joined by an inseparable bond to the saving work of her Son. In her the Church holds up and ad-

mires the most excellent fruit of the redemption, and joyfully contemplates, as in a faultless image, that which she herself desires and hopes wholly to be.

104. The Church has also included in the annual cycle days devoted to the memory of the martyrs and the other saints. Raised up to perfection by the manifold grace of God, and already in possession of eternal salvation, they sing God's perfect praise in heaven and offer prayers for us. By celebrating the passage of these saints from earth to heaven the Church proclaims the paschal mystery achieved in the saints who have suffered and been glorified with Christ; she proposes them to the faithful as examples drawing all to the Father through Christ, and through their merits she pleads for God's favors.

105. Finally, in the various seasons of the year and according to her traditional discipline, the Church completes the formation of the faithful by means of pious practices for soul and body, by instruction, prayer, and works of penance and of mercy.

Accordingly the sacred Council has seen fit to decree as follows.

106. By a tradition handed down from the apostles which took its origin from the very day of Christ's resurrection, the Church celebrates the paschal mystery every eighth day; with good reason this, then, bears the name of the Lord's day or Sunday. For on this day Christ's faithful should come together into one place so that, by hearing the word of God and taking part in the Eucharist, they may call to mind the passion, the resurrection, and the glorification of the Lord Jesus, and may thank God who "has begotten them again, through the resurrection of Jesus Christ from the dead, unto a living hope" (1 *Pet.* 1:3). Hence the Lord's day is the original feast day, and it should be proposed to the piety of the faithful and

taught to them so that it may become in fact a day of joy and of freedom from work. Other celebrations, unless they be truly of greatest importance, shall not have precedence over the Sunday which is the foundation and kernel of the whole liturgical year.

107. The liturgical year is to be revised so that the traditional customs and discipline of the sacred seasons shall be preserved or restored to suit the conditions of modern times; their specific character is to be retained, so that they duly nourish the piety of the faithful who celebrate the mysteries of Christian redemption, and above all the paschal mystery. If certain adaptations are considered necessary on account of local conditions, they are to be made in accordance with the provisions of Art. 39 and 40.

108. The minds of the faithful must be directed primarily toward the feasts of the Lord whereby the mysteries of salvation are celebrated in the course of the year. Therefore, the proper of the time shall be given the preference which is its due over the feasts of the saints, so that the entire cycle of the mysteries of salvation may be suitably recalled.

109. The season of Lent has a twofold character: primarily by recalling or preparing for baptism and by penance, it disposes the faithful, who more diligently hear the word of God and devote themselves to prayer, to celebrate the paschal mystery. This two-fold character is to be brought into greater prominence both in the liturgy and by liturgical catechesis. Hence:

(a) More use is to be made of the baptismal features proper to the Lenten liturgy; some of them, which used to flourish in bygone days, are to be restored as may seem good.

(b) The same is to apply to the penitential elements. As regards instruction it is important to impress on the minds of the faithful not only the social consequences of sin but

213

also that essence of the virtue of penance which leads to the detestation of sin as an offence against God; the role of the Church in penitential practices is not to be passed over, and the people must be exhorted to pray for sinners.

110. During Lent penance should not be only internal and individual, but also external and social. The practice of penance should be fostered in ways that are possible in our own times and in different regions, and according to the circumstances of the faithful; it should be encouraged by the authorities mentioned in Art. 22.

Nevertheless, let the paschal fast be kept sacred. Let it be celebrated everywhere on Good Friday and, where possible, prolonged throughout Holy Saturday, so that the joys of the Sunday of the resurrection may be attained with uplifted and clear mind.

111. The saints have been traditionally honored in the Church and their authentic relics and images held in veneration. For the feasts of the saints proclaim the wonderful works of Christ in His servants, and display to the faithful fitting examples for their imitation.

Lest the feasts of the saints should take precedence over the feasts which commemorate the very mysteries of salvation, many of them should be left to be celebrated by a particular Church or nation or family of religious; only those should be extended to the universal Church which commemorate saints who are truly of universal importance.

Chapter VI

Sacred Music

112. The musical tradition of the universal Church is a treasure of inestimable value, greater even than that of any other art. The main reason for this pre-eminence is that, as sacred song united to the words, it forms a necessary or integral part of the solemn liturgy.

Holy Scripture, indeed, has bestowed praise upon sacred song,[42] and the same may be said of the fathers of the Church and of the Roman pontiffs who in recent times, led by St. Pius X, have explained more precisely the ministerial function supplied by sacred music in the service of the Lord.

Therefore sacred music is to be considered the more holy in proportion as it is more closely connected with the liturgical action, whether it adds height to prayer, fosters unity of minds, or confers greater solemnity upon the sacred rites. But the Church approves of all forms of true art having the needed qualities, and admits them into divine worship.

Accordingly, the sacred Council, keeping to the norms and precepts of ecclesiastical tradition and discipline, and having regard to the purpose of sacred music, which is the glory of God and the sanctification of the faithful, decrees as follows.

113. Liturgical worship is given a more noble form when the divine offices are celebrated solemnly in song, with the assistance of sacred ministers and the active participation of the people.

As regards the language to be used, the provisions of Art. 36 are to be observed; for the Mass, Art. 54; for the sacraments, Art. 63; for the divine office, Art. 101.

114. The treasure of sacred music is to be preserved and fostered with great care. Choirs must be diligently promoted, especially in cathedral churches; but bishops and other pastors of souls must be at pains to ensure that, whenever the sacred action is to be celebrated with song, the whole body of the faithful may be able to contribute that active participation which is rightly theirs, as laid down in Art. 28 and 30.

115. Great importance is to be attached to the teaching and practice of music in seminaries, in the novitiates and houses of study of religious of both sexes, and also in other Catholic institutions and schools. To impart this instruction, teachers are to be carefully trained and put in charge of the teaching of sacred music.

It is desirable also to found higher institutes of sacred music whenever this can be done.

Composers and singers, especially boys, must also be given a genuine liturgical training.

116. The Church acknowledges Gregorian chant as especially suited to the Roman liturgy: therefore, other things being equal, it should be given pride of place in liturgical services.

But other kinds of sacred music, especially polyphony, are by no means excluded from liturgical celebrations, so long as they accord with the spirit of the liturgical action, as laid down in Art. 30.

117. The typical edition of the books of Gregorian chant

is to be completed; and a more critical edition is to be prepared of those books already published since the restoration by St. Pius X.

It is desirable also that an edition be prepared containing simpler melodies, for use in small churches.

118. Religious singing by the people is to be skillfully fostered, so that in devotions and sacred exercises, as also during liturgical services, the voices of the faithful may ring out according to the norms and requirements of the rubrics.

119. In certain parts of the world, especially mission lands, there are peoples who have their own musical traditions, and these play a great part in their religious and social life. For this reason due importance is to be attached to their music, and a suitable place is to be given to it, not only in forming their attitude toward religion, but also in adapting worship to their native genius, as indicated in Art. 39 and 40.

Therefore, when missionaries are being given training in music, every effort should be made to see that they become competent in promoting the traditional music of these peoples, both in schools and in sacred services, as far as may be practicable.

120. In the Latin Church the pipe organ is to be held in high esteem, for it is the traditional musical instrument which adds a wonderful splendor to the Church's ceremonies and powerfully lifts up man's mind to God and to higher things.

But other instruments also may be admitted for use in divine worship, with the knowledge and consent of the competent territorial authority, as laid down in Art. 22, §2, 37, and 40. This may be done, however, only on condition that the instruments are suitable, or can be made suitable, for sacred use, accord with the dignity of the temple, and truly contribute to the edification of the faithful.

121. Composers, filled with the Christian spirit, should

feel that their vocation is to cultivate sacred music and increase its store of treasures.

Let them produce compositions which have the qualities proper to genuine sacred music, not confining themselves to works which can be sung only by large choirs, but providing also for the needs of small choirs and for the active participation of the entire assembly of the faithful.

The texts intended to be sung must always be in conformity with Catholic doctrine; indeed they should be drawn chiefly from holy scripture and from liturgical sources.

Chapter VII

Sacred Art
and Sacred Furnishings

122. **V**ery rightly the fine arts are considered to rank among the noblest activities of man's genius, and this applies especially to religious art and to its highest achievement, which is sacred art. These arts, by their very nature, are oriented toward the infinite beauty of God which they attempt in some way to portray by the work of human hands; they achieve their purpose of redounding to God's praise and glory in proportion as they are directed the more exclusively to the single aim of turning men's minds devoutly toward God.

Holy Mother Church has therefore always been the friend of the fine arts and has ever sought their noble help, with the special aim that all things set apart for use in divine worship should be truly worthy, becoming, and beautiful, signs and symbols of the supernatural world, and for this purpose she has trained artists. In fact, the Church has, with good reason, always reserved to herself the right to pass judgment upon the arts, deciding which of the works of artists are in accordance with faith, piety, and cherished traditional laws, and thereby fitted for sacred use.

The Church has been particularly careful to see that sacred furnishings should worthily and beautifully serve the dignity of worship, and has admitted changes in materials, style, or ornamentation prompted by the progress of the technical arts with the passage of time.

Wherefore it has pleased the Fathers to issue the following decrees on these matters.

123. The Church has not adopted any particular style of art as her very own; she has admitted styles from every period according to the natural talents and circumstances of peoples, and the needs of the various rites. Thus, in the course of the centuries, she has brought into being a treasury of art which must be very carefully preserved. The art of our own days, coming from every race and region, shall also be given free scope in the Church, provided that it adorns the sacred buildings and holy rites with due reverence and honor; thereby it is enabled to contribute its own voice to that wonderful chorus of praise in honor of the Catholic faith sung by great men in times gone by.

124. Ordinaries, by the encouragement and favor they show to art which is truly sacred, should strive after noble beauty rather than mere sumptuous display. This principle is to apply also in the matter of sacred vestments and ornaments.

Let bishops carefully remove from the house of God and from other sacred places those works of artists which are repugnant to faith, morals, and Christian piety, and which offend true religious sense either by depraved forms or by lack of artistic worth, mediocrity and pretense.

And when churches are to be built, let great care be taken that they be suitable for the celebration of liturgical services and for the active participation of the faithful.

125. The practice of placing sacred images in churches so that they may be venerated by the faithful is to be main-

tained. Nevertheless their number should be moderate and their relative positions should reflect right order. For otherwise they may create confusion among the Christian people and foster devotion of doubtful orthodoxy.

126. When passing judgment on works of art, local ordinaries shall give a hearing to the diocesan commission on sacred art and, if needed, also to others who are especially expert, and to the commissions referred to in Art. 44, 45, and 46.

Ordinaries must be very careful to see that sacred furnishings and works of value are not disposed of or dispersed; for they are the ornaments of the house of God.

127. Bishops should have a special concern for artists, so as to imbue them with the spirit of sacred art and of the sacred liturgy. This they may do in person or through suitable priests who are gifted with a knowledge and love of art.

It is also desirable that schools or academies of sacred art should be founded in those parts of the world where they would be useful, so that artists may be trained.

All artists who, prompted by their talents, desire to serve God's glory in holy Church, should ever bear in mind that they are engaged in a kind of sacred imitation of God the Creator, and are concerned with works destined to be used in Catholic worship, to edify the faithful, and to foster their piety and their religious formation.

128. Along with the revision of the liturgical books, as laid down in Art. 25, there is to be an early revision of the canons and ecclesiastical statutes which govern the provision of material things involved in sacred worship. These laws refer especially to the worthy and well planned construction of sacred buildings, the shape and construction of altars, the nobility, placing, and safety of the Eucharistic tabernacle, the dignity and suitability of the baptistery, the proper or-

dering of sacred images, embellishments, and vestments. Laws which seem less suited to the reformed liturgy are to be brought into harmony with it, or else abolished; and any which are helpful are to be retained if already in use, or introduced where they are lacking.

According to the norm of Art. 22 of this Constitution, the territorial bodies of bishops are empowered to adapt such things to the needs and customs of their different regions; this applies especially to the materials and form of sacred furnishings and vestments.

129. During their philosophical and theological studies, clerics are to be taught about the history and development of sacred art, and about the sound principles governing the production of its works. In consequence they will be able to appreciate and preserve the Church's venerable monuments, and be in a position to aid, by good advice, artists who are engaged in producing works of art.

130. It is fitting that the use of pontificals be reserved to those ecclesiastical persons who have episcopal rank or some particular jurisdiction.

A Declaration
of the Second Ecumenical Council
of the Vatican on Revision
of the Calendar

The Second Ecumenical Council of the Vatican, recognizing the importance of the wishes expressed by many concerning the assignment of the feast of Easter to a fixed Sunday and concerning an unchanging calendar, having carefully considered the effects which could result from the introduction of a new calendar, declares as follows:

1. The sacred Council would not object if the feast of Easter were assigned to a particular Sunday of the Gregorian Calendar, provided that those whom it may concern, especially the brethren who are not in communion with the Apostolic See, give their assent.

2. The sacred Council likewise declares that it does not oppose efforts designed to introduce a perpetual calendar into civil society.

But, among the various systems which are being suggested to stabilize a perpetual calendar and to introduce it into civil life, the Church has no objection only in the case of those systems which retain and safeguard a seven-day week with Sunday, without the introduction of any days outside the week, so that the succession of weeks may be left intact, unless there is question of the most serious reasons. Concerning these the Apostolic See shall judge.

Notes

[1] Secret of the ninth Sunday after Pentecost.

[2] Cf. *Heb.* 13:14.

[3] Cf. *Eph.* 2:21-22.

[4] Cf. *Eph.* 4:13.

[5] Cf. *Is.* 11:12.

[6] Cf. *John* 11:52.

[7] Cf. *John* 10:16.

[8] Cf. *Is.* 61:1; Luke 4:18.

[9] St. Ignatius of Antioch, *To the Ephesians,* 7, 2.

[10] Cf. 1 *Tim.* 2:5.

[11] *Sacramentarium Veronese* (ed. Mohlberg), n. 1265; cf. also n. 1241, 1248.

[12] Easter Preface of the Roman Missal.

[13] Prayer before the second lesson for Holy Saturday, as it was in the Roman Missal before the restoration of Holy Week.

[14] Cf. *Mark* 16:15.

[15] Cf. *Acts* 26:18.

[16] Cf. *Rom.* 6:4; *Eph.* 2:6; *Col.* 3:1; 2 *Tim.* 2:11.

[17] Cf. *John* 4:23.

[18] Cf. 1 *Cor.* 11:26.

[19] Council of Trent, Session XIII, Decree on the Holy Eucharist, c. 5.

[20] Council of Trent, Session XXII, Doctrine on the Holy Sacrifice of the Mass, c. 2.

[21] Cf. St. Augustine, *Tractatus in Ioannem,* VI, n. 7.

[22] Cf. *Apoc.* 21:2; *Col.* 3:1; *Heb.* 8:2.

[23] Cf. *Phil.* 3:20; *Col.* 3:4.

[24] Cf. *John* 17:3; *Luke* 24:27; *Acts* 2:38.

[25] Cf. *Matt.* 28:20.

[26] Postcommunion for both Masses of Easter Sunday.

[27] Collect of the Mass for Tuesday of Easter Week.

[28] Cf. 2 *Cor.* 6:1.

[29] Cf. *Matt.* 6:6.

[30] Cf. 1 *Thess.* 5:17.

[31] Cf. 2 *Cor.* 4:10-11.

[32] Secret for Monday of Pentecost Week.

[33] St. Cyprian, *On the Unity of the Catholic Church*, 7; cf. Letter 66, n. 8, 3.

[34] Cf. Council of Trent, Session XXII, Doctrine on the Holy Sacrifice of the Mass, c. 8.

[35] Cf. St. Ignatius of Antioch, *To the Smyrnians*, 8; *To the Magnesians*, 7; *To the Philadelphians*, 4.

[36] Cf. St. Augustine, *Tractatus in Ioannem*, VI, n. 13.

[37] Roman Breviary, feast of Corpus Christi, Second Vespers, antiphon to the Magnificat.

[38] Cf. St. Cyril of Alexandria, *Commentary on the Gospel of John*, book XI, chap. XI-XII: Migne, *Patrologia Graeca*, 74, 557-564.

[39] Cf. 1 *Tim.* 2:1-2.

[40] Session XXI, July 16, 1562. Doctrine on Communion under Both Species, chap. 1-3: *Concilium Tridentinum. Diariorum, Actorum, Epistolarum, Tractatuum nova collectio*, ed. Soc. Goerresiana, tome VIII (Freiburg in Br., 1919), 698-699.

[41] Council of Trent, Session XXIV, November 11, 1563, On Reform, chap. I. Cf. Roman Ritual, title VIII, chap. II, n. 6.

[42] Cf. *Eph.* 5:19; *Col.* 3:16.

Appendix to the Constitution on the Sacred Liturgy *

(*Being excerpts from the* Declarations *added to the* Schema *prepared by the Preparatory Commission, for a clearer explanation of some of the articles.*)

On article 104 (now 128) of the Schema: (Declaration). *In surveying all the various external things which pertains to sacred worship, the following have been thought specially worthy of mention.*

1. *On the Preparation of the Church for the Sacred Liturgy*

The church edifice should be so arranged that the very position of all its elements and places should be a clear sign and a fatihful echo of the sacred liturgy, which is the assemblage of God's people hierarchically constituted and duly organized from His "servants" and His "holy people" (*Canon*

* Translated by HERBERT MUSURILLO, S.J., associate professor of classics, Fordham University, New York City.

of the Mass). The altar therefore should be carefully erected according to the requirements of the restored liturgy, especially in churches which are to be newly built, and there should also be a *sedes Episcopalis* (if necessary) and seats for the priests, seats or benches for the ministers, lecterns or reading stands for the singing of the sacred lessons, a place for the organ and the *schola cantorum,* places for the faithful, by which they "might be able to participate with better vision as well as spirit."

2. *On the Sedes Praesidentiales*

In cathedral churches, there should be a place set aside in the middle of the apse (which is at the front of the church or the congregation) for the bishop's throne that he might clearly appear as the bishop, and the ordinary one to preside over the liturgy. On both sides of the throne there should be seats for canons and priests. In other churches, where there is no episcopal throne, especially in parish churches, the place or honor can be filled by a simple chair for the pastor or the officiating priest, who presides over the liturgy in the name of the bishop, whose collaborator he is. However any suggestion of a throne should be avoided in those cases where the episcopal throne is not permitted.

3. *On the Main Altar*

The main altar, which is to be separated from the wall precisely that the ministers might easily walk around it, should fittingly be erected in a spot midway between the seats of the clergy and those of the faithful, that is to say in the middle of the church, although this is to be taken in a broad and not mathematical sense. So far as the nature of the building will allow, it would be praiseworthy for this altar to be covered with a *ciborium* or baldachino, that the

227

altar's sanctity might be thereby more manifest. Rectors of churches should recall that the altar is the place of the Eucharistic sacrifice and the venerable table for the sacred banquet; hence it should be decorated in a noble simple style, and anything that is foreign to the eucharistic cult should be strictly avoided. The crucifix and candles, required according to the liturgical quality of the Mass, should be placed either upon the altar, or even adjacent (around) the altar according to the earliest ecclesiastical usage.

4. *On the side altars*

The side altars should be so placed that they do not interfere with the liturgy which takes place around the main altar. In fact, insofar as the structure of the building and circumstances allow, they are better placed in special chapels rather than in the main body of the church.

5. *On the consecration of the Altar*

In addition to the main altar, which should always be a fixed altar, it is fitting that the side altars also be fixed and made of stone, unless the nature of the place (as for example in smaller oratories) precludes this. The manner of consecration should, if it can conveniently be done, follow that of the Roman *Pontificale,* which envisages the sacred relics being placed in the base, or even according to the oldest usage, underneath the altar itself. This avoids defacing the altar table unnecessarily, as occurs when the place of the relics is hollowed out of the top. The most fitting way is for the smooth altar top to be decorated alone with the crosses of consecration. Although a complete return to the ancient custom of the church of Rome is hardly feasible ("Let not the martyr be disturbed"; *Codex Theod.* 1.9, tit. 17 et 7; Braun,

Altar, I, 614), at the same time it is desirable that the relics of the saints to be placed in the altars be not too tiny. Above all it seems worthy of mature consideration whether or not, at least in certain cases, the custom may be started of consecrating particularly side altars (and, above all, portable altars) without relics. It woud seem that the practice of displaying make-believe bodies of saints, even though they may be joined with a few small authentic pieces, should be discontinued.

6. *On the Reservation of the Holy Eucharist*

The most Sacred Eucharist should regularly be reserved in a very solid and secure tabernacle, either on the main altar or else on a truly pre-eminent secondary altar, or, according to local or regional customs, in some other place in the church which is dignified and has been properly decorated. The sacrifice of the Mass should be permitted facing the people on a suitable altar, even though there may be a small tabernacle in the middle (one, however, which is of good material and dignified) where the Blessed Sacrament is reserved.

Especially in larger churches, it sometimes seems more fitting to have a special chapel of the Eucharist rather extensively decorated, either because of its antiquity or special artistic merits. Such a chapel is usually closed to mere spectators but open to worshippers, and can be better guarded against the danger of sacrilege.

7. *On the lecterns or reading stands*

In churches that are to be built, lecterns or reading stands for the singing of the sacred lessons should be so disposed that the majesty and dignity of the sacred Scriptures and indeed of God's word should be clearly proclaimed.

8. *On the place of the choir or schola cantorum*

The place for the choir or the schola cantorum should be so disposed that it might be clear that those who sing in the choir truly exercise an ecclesiastical function. In arranging its location, provision should always be made that individual choir members might easily receive Holy Communion.

9. *On the Place of the Faithful*

It is desirable that benches or seats should be regularly put out for the use of the faithful. We disapprove of the custom of reserving special places for individuals, for personal honors of this sort are to be avoided.

10. *On the Baptistery*

There should be a special place of honor for the baptistery in both cathedral and parish churches. It is desirable that the baptismal font should be so arranged that the baptism may be performed over it. If it can conveniently be done, the baptistery should be spacious and worthily arranged for the instruction of the faithful like a small room (*ad modum aulae*) so that both the sacred place and its ornaments might be a help to their initiation.

11. *On Confessionals*

The confessionals should be in a dignified spot, open and plain to see. They should fit in with the architecture of the church and be worthy of the admiration of the sacrament of Penance. Temporary confessionals, so far as possible, and those composed of a simple bench, should be avoided. Confessionals intended for men, in the form of small rooms near the sacristy, should be retained! [1]

12. *On Sacred Images*

From the earliest times the Catholic Church has always given a special honorific place in its edifices to sacred images, especially those of Our Lord Jesus Christ, then of the Blessed Virgin Mary Mother of God, of the Apostles and all the other saints; by these images she has offered veneration, and through them aroused and encouraged the piety of the faithful. In the arrangement of images, however, in churches and oratories, the sacred order should be rigorously adhered to. All images of Christ deserve a special place of honor at the very front of the church: that is, images of Christ incarnate, suffering, crucified, risen, ascending into heaven, in glorious triumph, seated at the right hand of the Father, and returning again in glory; so that, even though behind the main altar there may be permitted the titular image of the particular church or altar, at the same time the image of Christ should have the more important position. Without serious reason images of the same saints should not be multiplied within the same church building; the multiplication of such images behind the main altar is altogether disapproved of.

13. *On the Order of Decoration*

Since the function of painting and sculpture in the adornment of sacred buildings is twofold, namely decorative and

[1] TRANSLATOR'S NOTE. The meaning of this sentence will become clear if we examine the prescription on confessionals in the *Codex of Canon Law*, can. 909 § 1: "Confessionals for the hearing of woman's confessions should always be located in an open and conspicuous spot," where the same words are used as in our text. Cf. also can. 910 § 2: "The confessions of men may also be heard in private buildings."

iconographic, we must always seek a balance between the two, as well as between the realistic and the abstract, so that in all things the splendor of order might shine forth. In the decoration of sacred buildings the most important parts should in general have the more precious adornment.

14. *On Cemetery Art*

The faithful should be persuaded that in arranging for funerals and funeral monuments they should keep close to the concept of Christian death and eternal life, and should reject any appearance of superstition or pagan symbolism.

APPENDIX THREE

The Proper Construction of Churches and Altars

**In Order to Facilitate
the Active Participation
of the Faithful**

Chapter V of the Vatican Liturgy Commission's Instruction, *implementing changes in the Mass and other forms of the liturgy recommended in the Vatican Council's* Constitution on the Sacred Liturgy. *This* Instruction *was issued by the Sacred Congregation of Rites, with the date of September 26, 1964, but made public October 16, 1964.*

I. THE ARRANGEMENT OF CHURCHES

90. In the new construction, repair, or adaptation of churches great care should be taken that they are suitable for the celebration of divine services according to the true nature of the services and for the active participation of the faithful (cf. Const., art. 124).

II. THE MAIN ALTAR

91. It is proper that the main altar be constructed, sep-

arately from the wall, so that one may go around it with ease and so that celebration may take place facing the people; it shall occupy a place in the sacred building which is truly central, so that the attention of the whole congregation of the faithful is spontaneously turned to it.

In choosing the materials for the construction or ornamentation of the altar, the prescription of law shall be observed.

Moreover the presbyterium or sanctuary area around the altar shall be of sufficient size that the sacred rites may be conveniently celebrated.

III. THE SEAT OF THE CELEBRANT AND MINISTERS

92. The seat for the celebrant and ministers, according to the structure of individual churches, shall be so placed that it may be easily seen by the faithful and that the celebrant may truly appear to preside over the entire community of the faithful.

Nevertheless, if the seat is placed behind the altar, the form of a throne is to be avoided, as this belongs to the bishop alone.

IV. MINOR ALTARS

93. The minor altars shall be few in number. In fact, to the extent permitted by the structure of the building, it is highly suitable that they be placed in chapels in some way separated from the principal part of the church.

V. ORNAMENTATION OF ALTARS

94. The cross and candlesticks, which are required on the altar for the individual liturgical services, may also, in accordance with the judgment of the local Ordinary, be placed next to it.

VI. THE RESERVATION OF THE MOST HOLY EUCHARIST

95. The most holy eucharist shall be reserved in a solid and inviolable tabernacle placed in the middle of the main altar or of a minor, but truly outstanding, altar, or, according to lawful customs and in particular cases to be approved by the local Ordinary, also in some other noble and properly adorned part of the church.

It is lawful to celebrate mass facing the people even if there is a tabernacle, small but suitable, on the altar.

VII. THE AMBO

96. It is fitting that there be an ambo for the proclamation of the sacred readings, so arranged that the ministers can be easily seen and heard by the faithful.

VIII. THE PLACE OF THE SCHOLA AND ORGAN

97. The places for the schola and the organ shall be so arranged that it will be clearly evident that the singers and the organist form a part of the united community of the faithful and so that they may fulfill their liturgical function more suitably.

IX. THE PLACES OF THE FAITHFUL

98. The places for the faithful shall be arranged with particular care, so that they may participate in the sacred celebrations visually and with proper spirit. It is desirable that ordinarily benches or seats be provided for their use. Nevertheless, the custom of reserving seats for certain private persons is to be reprobated, in accordance with art. 32 of the Constitution.

Care shall also be taken that the faithful may not only see the celebrant and the other ministers but may also hear them easily, with the use of present-day technical means.

X. BAPTISTRY

99. In the construction and ornamentation of the baptistry, care shall be taken that the dignity of the sacrament of baptism is clearly apparent and that the place is suitable for the community celebration of the sacrament (cf. Const., art. 27).

The present Instruction, prepared at the command of Pope Paul VI by the Commission for the Implementation of the Constitution on the Sacred Liturgy, was presented to His Holiness by James Cardinal Lercaro, president of the Commission.

The Holy Father, after having given due consideration to this Instruction, with the help of the above mentioned Commission and of this Sacred Congregation of Rites, in an audience granted to Arcadio Maria Cardinal Larraona, prefect of the Congregation, on Sept. 26, 1964, approved it in a special way as a whole and in its parts, confirmed it by his authority, and ordered it to be published, and to be diligently observed by all concerned, beginning the First Sunday of Lent, March 7, 1965.

All things to the contrary notwithstanding.
Rome, Sept. 26, 1964.

JAMES CARDINAL LERCARO
Archbishop of Bologna
President of the Commission
for the Implementation of the
Constitution on the Sacred
Liturgy

ARCADIO M. CARD. LARRAONA
Prefect of S.R.C.
HENRY DANTE
Titular Archbishop of
Carpasia
Secretary of S.R.C.

Notes

INTRODUCTION

1. Printed in the special issue (1964) of the *Herder Correspondence,* pp. 24-26.
2. *Encounter* (January, 1965).
3. John J. Jankauskas, *Our Tongues Were Loosed* (Westminster, Maryland: The Newman Press, 1965).
4. See *Cahiers d'Action Religieuse et Sociale* (February 15, 1965), p. 130.

CHAPTER ONE—CHANGES IN THE CHURCH

1. *St. Louis Review* (August 21, 1964), p. 3.
2. Charles Davis, *Liturgy and Doctrine* (New York: Sheed & Ward, 1961), p. 38.
3. Richard Cardinal Cushing, *Liturgy and Life,* Pastoral Letter, Boston, 1964, p. 4.
4. Father François Houtart, *The Challenge to Change* (New York: Sheed & Ward, 1964), p. 24.
5. Father Rock Caporale, S.J., *Vatican II: Last of the Councils* (Baltimore: Helicon, 1964), p. 179.
6. Father Daniel J. O'Hanlon, S.J., in *Current Trends in Theology,* edited by Donald J. Wolf, S.J., and James V. Schall, S.J. (New York: Doubleday & Company, 1965), p. 271.
7. "Language and Liturgy" in *The Month* (January, 1965), p. 45.

8. See Adrien Nocent, O.S.B., *The Future of the Liturgy* (New York: Herder & Herder, 1963), notes on pp. 89, 169.

9. Léon-Joseph Cardinal Suenens, *The Nun in the World* (Westminster, Maryland: The Newman Press, 1963), pp. v, 165.

10. I owe this insight to the religious sociologist Father Rock Caporale, S.J., who developed it in his doctoral dissertation at Columbia University, 1965, as well as in the volume mentioned in note 5: *Vatican II: Last of the Councils.*

11. Father Louis Bouyer, *Liturgical Piety* (University of Notre Dame Press, 1955).

12. Father Gerald Ellard, S.J., in his volume *The Mass in Transition* (St. Paul, Minnesota: Bruce Publishing Company, 1956).

13. See "Worship and the Word," in *America* (August 19, 1961), p. 624.

14. Also in *America* (August 19, 1961), p. 274.

15. Now obtainable from America Press, 106 W. 56th St., New York City, in a new edition for which I have written an introduction in the light of the Council's Constitution on the Sacred Liturgy.

16. Father H. A. Reinhold in *Bringing the Mass to the People* (Baltimore: Helicon, 1960), p. 24.

17. This indispensable work, *Missarum Sollemnia: The Mass of the Roman Rite,* appears in two forms: the two-volume edition (New York: Benziger Brothers, 1950–1955), and the one-volume edition prepared by Charles K. Riepe (New York: Benziger Brothers, 1959).

18. See Appendix A in *Bringing the Mass to the People* (as in note 16), pp. 104–6.

19. For a concise history of these several developments, see *The Liturgical Movement,* by the Sacerdotal Communi-

ties of St. Séverin of Paris and St. Joseph of Nice, Volume 115 of *The Twentieth Century Encyclopedia of Catholicism* (New York: Hawthorn Books, 1964).

CHAPTER TWO—THE WORD

1. *Of Sacraments and Sacrifice* (Collegeville, Minnesota: Liturgical Press, 1952) is the title of Father Clifford Howell's very influential work. Father Howell, it need hardly be said, has never understressed the importance of the Word; indeed, his gifts in presenting the Word are prodigious and internationally esteemed.

2. See Father Johannes Hofinger's *The Art of Teaching Christian Doctrine* (University of Notre Dame Press, 1962), p. 6, note 1, where a full bibliography on the subject is given.

3. For the history of this controversy, see Joseph A. Jungmann's *Handing on the Faith* (New York: Herder & Herder, 1959), Appendix III, pp. 398–405; also Karl Rahner's *Theology for Renewal* (New York: Sheed & Ward, 1965), pp. 144–46.

4. See, for example, two superlative series of textbooks, both in the *Lumen Vitae* tradition: *Lord and King*, by Vincent Novak, S.J., and associates (New York: Holt, Rinehart & Winston, 1964), and *Christ Teaches Us Today*, by Mark Link, S.J. (Chicago: Loyola University Press, 1964). See also the proceedings of the Twenty-Fourth North American Liturgical Week, *The Renewal of Christian Education* (Liturgical Conference, 1963).

5. Father Domenico Grasso's "Kerygma and Preaching" in *The Word: Readings in Theology* (New York: P. J. Kenedy & Sons, 1964), p. 230.

6. In *Teaching All Nations,* edited by Johannes Hofinger, S.J. (New York: Herder & Herder, 1961).

7. Charles Merrill Smith in *How to Become a Bishop Without Being Religious* (New York: Doubleday & Company, 1965).

8. Reprinted in *The Challenge of the Council* (Liturgical Conference, 1964), pp. 217–20.

9. Published in *The Assisi Papers* (Collegeville, Minnesota: Liturgical Press, 1957). This point has been further developed by Father R. A. F. MacKenzie, S.J., in his *Introduction to the New Testament* (Liturgical Press, 1960), p. 40; and by Father David M. Stanley, S.J., in his essay "The Fonts of Preaching" in *Liturgy for the People* (St. Paul, Minnesota: Bruce Publishing Company, 1963), pp. 21–28.

10. "Reform of the Religious Life Through the Liturgy" is a very challenging chapter in Father George Tavard's volume, *The Church Tomorrow* (New York: Herder & Herder, 1965).

11. In *The Word: Readings in Theology,* compiled at the Canisianum, Innsbruck (New York: P. J. Kenedy & Sons, 1964).

12. Hans Urs von Balthasar, *Word and Revelation* (New York: Herder & Herder, 1964), p. 28.

13. Cited in *The Word: Readings in Theology* (New York: P. J. Kenedy & Sons, 1964), p. 186.

14. Romano Guardini, *Meditations Before Mass* (Westminster, Maryland: The Newman Press, 1955), pp. 5, 10–11.

15. A volume that deserves to be the *vade mecum* of every parish priest is *Sunday Morning Crisis,* edited by Father Robert W. Hovda (Baltimore, Maryland: Helicon, 1963). Though prepared before the Constitution was promul-

gated, everything in this book is in line with the Constitution's spirit. Further, it is by no means limited to short-range solutions; rather, it explores the meaning of parish worship in depth.

16. H. Marshall McLuhan's explosive books, the *Gutenberg Galaxy* (University of Toronto Press, 1962), and *Understanding Media* (New York: McGraw-Hill, 1964) and 1965 in paperback (McGraw-Hill), challenge most of our preconceptions on the subject and make useful material for study by liturgists and others concerned about preaching and homiletics.

17. My own treatments may be found in "The Language of Prayer," in *Liturgy for the People*, edited by William Leonard, S.J. (St. Paul, Minnesota: Bruce Publishing Company, 1963), pp. 91–103; and in several articles: "The Vernacular Re-Viewed," in *Worship* (March, 1961), pp. 241–50 (reprints of this appeared in pamphlet form under the same title, published by the Liturgical Press, Collegeville, Minnesota, and in the *Catholic Mind* for May–June, 1961); "Should the Mass Be in English?" in *America* (December 16, 1961), pp. 387–390; in *The 2nd Vatican Council* (New York: America Press, 1962), "The Liturgy and the Council," pp. 36–42. Father Angelus A. De Marco's volume *Rome and the Vernacular* (Westminster, Maryland: The Newman Press, 1961), and Paul Winninger's *Langues Vivantes et Liturgie* (Paris: Les Editions du Cerf, 1961) should be read by anyone interested in the problem or disturbed by it.

18. See Professor G. B. Harrison's magisterial article, "Words to Pray With?" in *America* (April 11, 1964), pp. 508–10, and my own treatments of the subject, in *America* (December 16, 1961), p. 387, and *Worship* (March, 1961), pp. 249–50.

19. See any recent study of language or poetry, like Remy C. Kwant's *Phenomenology of Language* (Duquesne University Press, 1965), or the works of C. E. Osgood, G. J. Suci and P. H. Tanenbaum in *The Measurement of Meaning* (University of Illinois Press, 1957), as well as some of the literature in contemporary linguistics.

20. In *American Psychologist* (January, 1965), pp. 34–50.

21. *The Clergy Review* (January, 1965), p. 67.

22. Karl Rahner, *Theological Investigations,* Vol. II: *Man in the Church* (Baltimore: Helicon, 1964), p. 175.

23. See Rock Caporale, *Vatican II: Last of the Councils* (as before in note 5, Chapter One), especially Chapter 14.

24. Otto Semmelroth, S.J., *The Preaching Word* (New York: Herder & Herder, 1965), p. 131; see also pp. 226–37. This is the place to recommend *The Bible Today,* published six times a year by the Liturgical Press, Collegeville, Minnesota, and such books as *Foundations of Biblical Spirituality,* by several Scriptural theologians like Stanislas Lyonnet and Gaston Salet, translated by Joseph A. Grispino, S.M. (Staten Island, New York: Alba House, 1965).

CHAPTER THREE—SACRAMENTS AND SYMBOLS

1. Dom Anscar Vonier in his classic work, *A Key to the Doctrine of the Eucharist* (Westminster, Maryland: The Newman Press, 1956), p. 35.

2. See especially Ernst Cassirer's great three-volume work, *The Philosophy of Symbolic Forms* (Yale University Press, 1953, 1955, 1957), and several shorter works by Susanne K. Langer: *Philosophy in a New Key* (Harvard University Press and New York: New American Library, paperback), and *Philosophical Sketches* (Johns Hopkins,

1962, and New American Library paperback), notably the chapter "On a New Definition of 'Symbol.'" Mircea Eliade's studies of myth and symbol are very important, and his volume *Patterns in Comparative Religion* (New York: Sheed & Ward, 1958, and New York: Meridian Books, paperback) will serve as a good introduction to this aspect of liturgy.

3. "Christian Sacrament: Sign and Experience," published in *Participation in the Mass* (Twentieth North American Liturgical Week), p. 249. It would be hard to improve on Marshall McLuhan's description of symbol here: "Suppose that, instead of displaying the Stars and Stripes, we were to write the words 'American flag' across a piece of cloth and to display that. While the symbols would convey the same meaning, the effect would be quite different. To translate the rich visual mosaic of the Stars and Stripes into written form would be to deprive it of most of its qualities of corporate image and of experience, yet the abstract literal bond would remain much the same" (*Understanding Media,* p. 82). He also points out that "the new preference for depth participation has also prompted in the young a strong drive toward religious experience with rich liturgical overtones" (p. 321).

4. See Charles Davis' useful book, *Sacraments of Initiation* (New York: Sheed & Ward, 1964).

5. See *Sacraments of Initiation* (as above), pp. 141–42.

6. A lucid and very sound introduction to this whole subject may be found in Father John M. Miller's *Signs of Transformation in Christ* (Englewood Cliffs, New Jersey: Prentice-Hall, 1963).

7. See E. H. Gombrich's article, together with its full bibliography, referred to in Chapter Two's note 20.

8. See Father Tolland's article, "Christian Sacrament: Sign

and Experience," mentioned in note 3; especially pp. 252–53.

9. See Father Herbert Musurillo's *Symbolism and the Christian Imagination* (Baltimore: Helicon, 1962), p. 3; and Father Gerald Vann's *The Paradise Tree: On Living the Symbols of the Church* (New York: Sheed & Ward, 1959). Also the section "Universality of Symbols," in Mircea Eliade's great study *The Sacred and the Profane* (New York: Harcourt, Brace & World, 1957).

10. Vincent V. Herr, S.J., *Religious Psychology* (New York: Alba House, Staten Island, 1965), pp. 191–92.

11. Constitution on the Church, Articles 50 and 51.

12. To understand the implications of these sections of the Constitution, one can do no better than study the chapters "The Paschal Mystery" and "The Mystery of Worship" in Louis Bouyer's commentary, *The Liturgy Revived* (University of Notre Dame Press, paperback, 1965). And for further development of this difficult subject, I strongly recommend Chapter 4, "The Liturgy: Mystery of Worship," in I. H. Dalmais, O.P., *Introduction to the Liturgy* (Baltimore: Helicon, 1961). Father Charles K. Riepe's masterly little work, *Living the Christian Seasons* (New York: Herder & Herder, 1964), explains in untechnical language the meaning of Sunday and the interrelationship among seasons and feasts.

13. For a better understanding of eschatology, read the chapters "The Resurrection of the Body" and "The End of the World," in Charles Davis' *Theology for Today* (New York: Sheed & Ward, 1963).

14. I recommend strongly one of Father Karl Rahner's most stimulating chapters "The Sacramental Basis of the Layman" in *Nature and Grace: Dilemmas in the Modern Church* (New York: Sheed & Ward, 1964), pp. 83–113.

His general treatment of the sacraments in eschatological terms may be found in *Sendung und Gnade,* pp. 162–97.

15. Evelyn Underhill, *Worship* (New York: Harper & Row, 1937), p. 245. Also available in paperback (Harper & Row, 1957).

CHAPTER FIVE—SOCIAL MEANING OF THE LITURGY

1. Father Shawn G. Sheehan, "Apostolic Dimension of the Liturgy Course," a chapter in *Apostolic Renewal in the Seminary* (New York: The Christophers, 1965, pp. 204–5.

2. Father Henri de Lubac, *Catholicism,* first published in 1937 with the subtitle *The Social Aspects of Dogma.* Now available in paperback (New York: New American Library).

3. Most liturgical scholars stress the importance of this theme. See, for example, Louis Bouyer's chapter "From the Jewish Qahal to the Christian Ecclesia," in *Liturgical Piety* (University of Notre Dame Press, 1955), pp. 23–37; Eugene H. Maly's essay, "Israel—God's Liturgical People," in *Liturgy for the People: Essays in Honor of Father Gerald Ellard,* edited by William J. Leonard (St. Paul, Minnesota: Bruce Publishing Company, 1963), pp. 10–20; I. H. Dalmais' chapter, "The Christian Liturgical Assembly: the Church," in *Introduction to the Liturgy* (Baltimore: Helicon, 1961), pp. 27–37.

4. See also Charles Davis' *Liturgy and Doctrine* (New York: Sheed & Ward, 1961), especially the magnificent chapter "The Mass as the Assembly of Christians," pp. 323–47.

5. Reprinted in *The Renewal of Christian Education* (Liturgical Conference, 1963), pp. 35–43.

6. David M. Stanley, S.J., "The Fonts of Preaching," in *Liturgy for the People: Essays in Honor of Father Gerald Ellard,* edited by William J. Leonard (St. Paul, Minnesota: Bruce Publishing Company, 1963), pp. 23–24.

7. Maurice Nédoncelle, *God's Encounter with Man* (New York: Sheed & Ward, 1964), p. 145.

8. Dietrich von Hildebrand, *Liturgy and Personality* (Baltimore: Helicon, 1960), pp. 27, 34.

9. In *America* (February 27, 1965), p. 287.

10. In *Schriften,* by Karl Rahner, Vol. II, pp. 132–33; and Edward Shillebeeckx's *Christ, the Sacrament of the Encounter with God* (New York: Sheed & Ward, 1963), pp. 153–78.

11. Charles Davis, *The Sacraments of Initiation* (New York: Sheed & Ward, 1964), p. 148.

12. *The Sacraments of Initiation* (as above), pp. 174, 178, 179.

13. Father Philip Berrigan, S.S.J., "The Nature of Christian Witness," in *No More Strangers* (New York: The Macmillan Company, 1965).

14. See also Father Peter J. Riga's article, "Liturgy and Action," in *Commonweal* (Christmas issue, 1964).

15. See Charles Davis' exciting treatment of the sacrament of Penance in Chapter 18 of his *Theology for Today* (New York: Sheed & Ward, 1963).

16. Dietrich Bonhoeffer, *The Cost of Discipleship* (New York: The Macmillan Company, 1963), p. 285.

17. Karl Rahner, *The Christian Commitment* (New York: Sheed & Ward, 1963), pp. 59–60.

18. *The Christian Commitment* (as above), p. 11.

19. See Father Benjamin L. Masse's masterly introduction to the social teachings of the Church, *Justice for All* (St. Paul, Minnesota: Bruce Publishing Company, 1964).

20. Quoted by Ed Marciniak in "The Mass and Economic Order," in *Liturgy and Social Order* (Liturgical Conference, 1955), p. 117.

CHAPTER SIX—LITURGY AND ECUMENISM

1. See Christopher Dawson's most recent work, which gives the background of this vast subject, *The Dividing of Christendom* (New York: Sheed & Ward, 1965).
2. Remarks made at the symposium, "Ecumenism and the Modern World," held at Duquesne University, March 1-4, 1965.
3. See, for example, Albert Christ-Janer and Mary M. Foley, *Modern Church Architecture* (New York: McGraw Hill, 1962).
4. The concluding paragraph of his important volume, (Protestant) *Worship and Church Architecture* (New York: Oxford University Press, 1964), p. 201.
5. I have treated the subject briefly in *America* (February 29, 1964), in an article, "Liturgy—Barrier or Bond?"
6. Joseph Lortz, *How the Reformation Happened* (New York: Herder & Herder, 1964).
7. Session 22, canon 8.
8. See Theodor Klauser, *The Western Liturgy and Its History* (1952), and Professor Klauser's important lecture, *The Western Liturgy To-Day* (Westminster, Maryland: Canterbury Press, 1963). Another useful volume is Albert Mirgeler's *Mutations of Western Christianity* (New York: Herder & Herder, 1964), especially pp. 55–58, 62–65, 71, 104–6, and 138–40, where devotional and liturgical developments are clearly treated. (The word "rubric" refers to the detailed directives given for even the most minute ceremony of the liturgy.)

9. See Father Piet Fransen, S.J., "Sacraments: Signs of Faith," in *Worship* (December, 1962), and Father Cornelius Ernst, O.P., "Acts of Christ: Signs of Faith," in *Sacraments, the Gestures of Christ* (New York: Sheed & Ward, 1965).

10. Father Louis Bouyer's "The Sacramental System," in *Sacraments, the Gestures of Christ* (as above).

11. The phrase is J. D. Crichton's, in "An Historical Sketch of the Roman Liturgy," from *True Worship* (Baltimore: Helicon, 1964).

12. See Father Hendrik Manders' chapter, "Concelebration," in Vol. II of *Concilium: the Church and the Liturgy* Glen Rock, New Jersey: Paulist Press, 1965), and Father Herman Schmidt's bibliography, in the same volume, of seventy-five items on concelebration in the past sixty-five years.

13. Mother Jean C. McCowan, R.S.C.J. *Concelebration* (Herder & Herder, 1963). The article "Modes of Concelebration and Their Relative Value" was published in *The Challenge of the Council: Person, Parish, World* (Liturgical Conference, 1964).

14. Father Godfrey Diekmann's "The Full Sign of the Eucharist," p. 92 in the Liturgical Conference volume mentioned above.

15. Father Adrien Nocent, *The Future of the Liturgy* (New York: Herder & Herder, 1963), p. 177.

16. See A. G. Martimort, *The Signs of the New Covenant* (Collegeville, Minnesota: Liturgical Press, 1963), p. 172.

17. Dr. Cyril C. Richardson's "Word and Sacrament in Protestant Worship," in *Ecumenical Dialogue at Harvard: the Roman Catholic-Protestant Colloquium,* edited by Samuel H. Miller and G. Ernest Wright (Harvard University Press, 1964), p. 153.

18. I direct your attention to several books on the Protestant liturgical development mentioned in our bibliography, as well as to Dr. Ernest Koenker's study on the Catholic renewal as listed there.

19. This subject is brilliantly treated by Louis Bouyer in "Jewish and Christian Liturgies," Chapter 3 of Lancelot Sheppard's *True Worship* (Baltimore: Helicon, 1963), pp. 29–44.

20. Father Alexander Schemann, *Sacraments and Orthodoxy* (New York: Herder & Herder, 1965), p. 8.

CHAPTER SEVEN—LITURGY AND THE ARTS

1. Christopher Dawson, *The Dividing of Christendom* (New York: Sheed & Ward, 1965), p. 289.

2. I have treated this subject several times in *America* magazine. One such column, "What's a Church For?" appears on pp. 495–96 of the April 10, 1965, issue. In the article there is some discussion of an important meeting of liturgists and architects at Cleveland, and especially of Bernard Cooke's and Edward A. Sovik's very perceptive remarks.

3. I have discussed this at some length in an article, "The Priest as Patron," in *Liturgical Arts* (May, 1961); Father Thomas Mathews' article with the same title appeared in *America* (June 6, 1964) and treats the subject in greater depth and from several other angles.

4. I have treated the tensions implicit in the liturgy in a chapter of *The Revival of the Liturgy*, edited by Frederick R. McManus (New York: Herder & Herder, 1963), p. 163–90, where a fairly large bibliography on the subject is included.

5. A penetrating analysis of the meaning of the ambo, as well as of other architectural problems, is found in Father Godfrey Diekmann's chapter, "The Place of Liturgical Worship," in *The Church and the Liturgy* (Glen Rock, New Jersey: Concilium, 1965), Vol. II.

6. *The Church and the Liturgy* (as above), p. 105.

7. The best treatment I know of this subject is that of Father Thomas Mathews, S.J., a professional art historian: "Toward an Adequate Notion of Tradition in Sacred Art," *Liturgical Arts* (February, 1964).

8. The reader may find this treated at some length in the chapter referred to in note 4; the next few paragraphs will predictably bear some resemblance to this fuller discussion.

9. See *America* (November 21, 1964), p. 675. I am indebted to the patristic scholar Father James A. McDonough, S.J., and to the musicologist Dr. James McKinnon for some of the material used here.

10. In "Music and the Constitution" in *The Challenge of the Council: Person, Parish, World* (as in note 13 for Chapter Six), p. 208.

11. Printed in *America* (August 31, 1963). Since interviews with Stravinsky are rare, this one was rather widely reprinted in several foreign countries.

CHAPTER EIGHT—ANXIETIES ABOUT THE LITURGY

1. Odo Casel in *Le Mystère du culte dans le Christianisme* (Paris: Les Editions du Cerf, 1964), p. 48.

2. In *Worship* (February, 1965), pp. 67–68.

3. The Feasts of Mary and of the saints in terms of the

Redemption have been briefly and effectively explained in Father Charles Riepe's volume, *Living the Christian Seasons* (New York: Herder & Herder, 1964), pp. 67–69, 85–87.

4. Karl Rahner, *Schriften,* Vol. 3, pp. 400–10.

5. See also Father David M. Stanley's chapter, "From His Heart Will Flow Rivers of Living Water," in *Cor Jesu* (New York: Herder & Herder, 1959), Vol. I, pp. 509–42.

6. Charles Davis, "The Theology of Transubstantiation" in *Sophia* (April, 1964); summarized in *The Downside Review* (January, 1965).

7. Karl Rahner, S.J., *The Christian Commitment* (New York: Sheed & Ward, 1963, pp. 142–45.

9. In his Ash Wednesday audience, March 3, 1965.

10. Chapter 5 in *True Worship* by Lancelot Sheppard (Baltimore: Helicon, 19).

11. Father Karl Rahner's "Developing Eucharistic Devotion," a chapter in *The Christian Commitment* (as in note 7), pp. 173, 176–77.

12. The *docetists* were members of an early heretical sect which held that Christ's body was merely a phantom or appearance, or that if real its substance was celestial. The *acosmists* denied the existence of the universe as distinct from God, and the *Pelagians* (followers of Pelagius, a British monk), denied original sin and held that man has perfect freedom of will.

13. Quoted by Henri de Lubac, S.J., in *La pensée religieuse du Père Teilhard de Chardin* (Paris: Aubier, 1962), p. 339.

Suggested Reading

INTRODUCTION

Josef A. Jungmann, S.J. *The Mass of the Roman Rite,* one-volume edition prepared by Charles K. Riepe. New York: Benziger Brothers, 1959.

The Church and the Liturgy, Concilium, Vol. II. Glen Rock, New Jersey: Paulist Press, 1965.

Gerald Ellard, S.J. *The Mass of the Future.* St. Paul, Minnesota: Bruce Publishing Company, 1948.

———. *The Mass in Transition.* St. Paul, Minnesota: Bruce Publishing Company, 1956.

Adrien Nocent, O.S.B. *The Future of the Liturgy.* New York: Herder & Herder, 1963.

John D. Crichton. *The Church's Worship.* New York: Sheed & Ward, 1964.

William J. Leonard, S.J. *New Horizons in Catholic Worship,* arranged for study by Monsignor Leon A. McNeill. Liturgical Commission, 445 N. Emporia, Wichita, Kansas, 1965.

———. *New Horizons in Liturgical Living.* Liturgical Commission, 1965.

John J. Jankauskas. *Our Tongues Were Loosed.* Westminster, Maryland: The Newman Press, 1965.

The Liturgical Movement, by the Sacerdotal Communities of Saint-Séverin of Paris and St. Joseph of Nice. New York: Hawthorn Books, 1964.

C. J. McNaspy, S.J. Introduction and commentary accompanying the authorized translation of the Constitution on the Sacred Liturgy in the collection of all the documents: *Documents of Vatican II.* New York: Guild Press, 1966.

H. A. Reinhold. *Bringing the Mass to the People.* Baltimore: Helicon Books, 1960.

Theodor Klauser. *The Wesern Liturgy To-Day.* Westminster, Maryland, 1963.

Donald J. Wolf and James V. Schall, S.J. (eds.). *Current Trends in Theology.* New York: Doubleday & Company, 1965.

Angelus A. De Marco, O.F.M. *A Key to the New Liturgical Constitution.* New York: Desclee Company, 1964.

Louis Bouyer. *The Liturgy Revived.* University of Notre Dame Press, paperback, 1965.

Frederick R. McManus. *The Council and the Liturgy.* Washington, D.C.: National Catholic Welfare Conference, paperback, 1965.

Godfrey Diekmann, O.S.B. *Come Let Us Worship.* Baltimore: Helicon Books, 1961.

James W. King, S.J. *The Liturgy and the Laity.* Westminster, Maryland: The Newman Press, 1963.

H. A. Reinhold. *The Dynamics of Liturgy.* New York: The Macmillan Company, 1961.

Charles Davis. *Liturgy and Doctrine.* New York: Sheed & Ward, 1960.

Louis Bouyer. *Liturgical Piety.* University of Notre Dame Press, 1957.

I. H. Dalmais, O.P. *Introduction to the Liturgy.* Baltimore: Helicon Books, 1961.

CHAPTER ONE

Archbishop Paul J. Hallinan. *How to Understand Changes in the Liturgy,* pamphlet available from P.O. Box 11667, Northside Station, Atlanta, Georgia.

Preaching the Liturgical Renewal, booklet with preface by H. A. Reinhold, Liturgical Conference, 1964.

Gerard S. Sloyan. *Liturgy in Focus.* Glen Rock, New Jersey: Deus Books, paperback, Paulist Press, 1964.

——. *To Hear the Word of God: Homilies at Mass.* New York: Herder & Herder, 1965.

Clifford Howell, S.J. *Of Sacraments and Sacrifice.* Collegeville, Minnesota: Liturgical Press, 1952.

Robert W. Hovda (ed.). *Sunday Morning Crisis.* Baltimore: Helicon Books, 1963.

Frederick R. McManus. *The Revival of the Liturgy.* New York: Herder & Herder, 1963.

William J. Leonard, S.J. (ed.). *Liturgy for the People.* St. Paul, Minnesota: Bruce Publishing Company, 1963.

Alfons Kirchgaessner (ed.). *Unto the Altar.* New York: Herder & Herder, 1963.

John H. Miller, C.S.C. *Fundamentals of the Liturgy.* University of Notre Dame Press, 1960.

Cipriano Vagaggini. *The Theological Dimensions of the Liturgy.* Collegeville, Minnesota: Liturgical Press, 1959.

Josef A. Jungmann, S.J. *Public Worship.* Collegeville, Minnesota: Liturgical Press, 1957.

CHAPTER TWO

Sofia Cavaletti and Gianna Gobbi. *Teaching Doctrine and Liturgy.* Staten Island, New York: Alba House, 1964.

Josef A. Jungmann, S.J. *Pastoral Liturgy*. New York: Herder & Herder, 1962.

———. *Handing on the Faith*. New York: Herder & Herder, 1959.

Johannes Hofinger, S.J. *The Art of Teaching Christian Doctrine*. University of Notre Dame Press, 1962.

Otto Semmelroth, S.J. *The Preaching Word*. New York: Herder & Herder, 1965.

Hans Urs von Balthasar. *Word and Revelation*. New York: Herder & Herder, 1964.

Vincent M. Novak, S.J., John Nelson, S.J., and collaborators. Textbook series of new catechetical method, New York: Fordham University Press, 1962–1965, 501 E. Fordham Road, Bronx 58.

Mark J. Link, S.J. *Christ Teaches Us Today*. Chicago: Loyola University Press, 1965.

CHAPTER THREE

John H. Miller, C.S.C. *Signs of Transformation in Christ*. Englewood Cliffs, New Jersey: Prentice-Hall, 1963.

A. M. Roguet, O.P. *The Sacraments, Signs of Life*. Collegeville, Minnesota: Liturgical Press, 1954.

———. *Christ Acts Through the Sacraments*. Collegeville, Minnesota: Liturgical Press, 1953.

Aimé Georges Martimort. *The Signs of the New Covenant*. Collegeville, Minnesota: Liturgical Press, 1963.

Louis Bouyer. *Rite and Man: Natural Sacredness and Christian Liturgy*, University of Notre Dame Press, 1963.

Karl Rahner, S.J. *The Church and the Sacraments*. New York: Herder & Herder, 1963.

———. *Nature and Grace*. New York: Sheed & Ward, 1963.

Francis X. Durrwell, C.SS.R. *The Resurrection*. New York: Sheed & Ward, 1960.

Denis O'Callaghan (ed.). *Sacraments, the Gestures of Christ.* New York: Sheed & Ward, 1964.

Edward Schillebeeckx, O.P. *Christ: The Sacrament of the Encounter with God.* New York: Sheed & Ward, 1963.

CHAPTER FIVE

Richard Cardinal Cushing. *Liturgy and Life.* Pastoral letter, Boston, 1964.

Liturgy and Social Order. Liturgical Conference, 1956.

Brian Wicker. *Culture and Liturgy.* New York: Sheed & Ward, 1963.

Karl Rahner, S.J. *The Christian Commitment.* New York: Sheed & Ward, 1963.

Philip Berrigan, S.S.J. *No More Strangers.* New York: The Macmillan Company, 1965.

Benjamin L. Masse, S.J. *Justice for All.* St. Paul, Minnesota: Bruce Publishing Company, 1965.

CHAPTER SIX

Romey P. Marshall, O.S.L., and Michael J. Taylor, S.J. *Liturgy and Christian Unity.* Englewood Cliffs, New Jersey: Prentice-Hall, 1965.

Alexander Schmemann. *Sacraments and Orthodoxy.* New York: Herder & Herder, 1965.

Michael J. Taylor, S.J. *The Protestant Liturgical Renewal.* Westminster, Maryland: The Newman Press, 1963.

James F. White. *Protestant Worship and Church Architecture.* New York: Oxford University Press, 1964.

Christopher Dawson. *The Dividing of Christendom.* New York: Sheed & Ward, 1965.

Massey Hamilton Shepherd, Jr. (ed.). *The Liturgical Renewal of the Church.* New York: Oxford University Press, 1960.

Ernest Benjamin Koenker. *The Liturgical Renaissance in the Roman Catholic Church.* University of Chicago Press, 1954.

William Nicholls. *Jacob's Ladder, The Meaning of Worship.* Richmond, Virginia: John Knox Press, 1964.

The Frozen and the Chosen. Lutheran Laymen's League, 1964.

CHAPTER SEVEN

Kevin Seasoltz, O.S.B. *Sacred Art and Architecture.* New York: Herder & Herder, 1963.

Pie-Raymond Régamey. *Religious Art in the Twentieth Century.* New York: Herder & Herder, 1963.

Gerardus van der Leeuw. *Sacred and Profane Beauty: The Holy in Art.* New York: Holt, Rinehart & Winston, 1963.

Paul Weiss. *Religion and Art.* Marquette University Press, 1963.

Albert Christ-Janer and Mary M. Foley. *Modern Church Architecture.* New York: McGraw-Hill, 1962.

Peter Hammond. *Liturgy and Architecture.* Columbia University Press, 1961; *Towards a Church Architecture.* New York: Architectural Book Publishing Company, 1962.

Eduard Syndicus, S.J. *Early Christian Art.* New York: Hawthorn Books, 1962.

Joseph Gelineau, S.J. *Voices and Instruments in Christian Worship.* New York: Liturgical Press, 1964.

Paul Hume. *Catholic Church Music.* New York: Dodd, Mead & Co., 1956.

Erik Routley. *Church Music and Theology.* Philadelphia: Fortress Press, 1959.

A Manual for Church Musicians. Collegeville, Minnesota: Liturgical Press, 1964.

CHAPTER EIGHT

Dietrich von Hildebrand. *Liturgy and Personality*. Baltimore: Helicon Books, 1960.

Josef Goldbrunner. *Holiness Is Wholeness and Other Essays*. University of Notre Dame Press, 1964.

Maurice Nédoncelle. *God's Encounter With Man*. New York: Sheed & Ward, 1964.

Mark J. Link, S.J. (ed.). *Teaching the Sacraments and Morality*. Chicago: Lumen Vitae-Loyola University Press, 1965.

Romano Guardini. *Meditations Before Mass*. Westminster, Maryland: The Newman Press, 1960.

Hans Urs von Balthasar. *Prayer*. New York: Sheed & Ward, 1963.

Hubert van Zeller, O.S.B. *The Mass in Other Words*. Templegate, Publishers, Box 963, Springfield, Illinois, 1965.

Pierre Teilhard de Chardin. *Hymn of the Universe*. New York: Harper & Row, 1965.

INDEX

Abbots, blessing of, 120, 197
Abraham, 99
Adaptation, 28, 71–72, 176, 190–92 (*see also* specific areas); and art, 222 (*see also* Art and furnishings); liturgical commissions and, 193; and liturgical year, 213; and music, 217 (*see also* Music)
Adolescence, and first communion, 17
Advent, Bible services in, 190
Aestheticism, 70, 71
African music, 144
Age (*see also* Old age); for Confirmation, 106
Agnostics at Solesmes, 146
Agnus Dei, 89, 93
Alleluia, 92, 148
Altamira, 127
Altars, 83, 135–37, 138, 164, 221, 227–29, 234–35; and concelebration (*see* Concelebration); in outline of new Mass, 86*ff*; position relative to lectern discussed by White, 113; Reformation and, 113
Ambos (lecterns), 71, 85, 138*ff*, 235. *See also* Lecterns
Ambrosian hymns, 58
America (periodical), 59
American Bishops' Commission, 80
Angelism, 70–71
Anglicans and Anglicanism, 62, 123, 167
Anointing of the Sick, 78–79, 109, 202–3
Apologists, 30–31
Apostles, 22, 109, 179; and Divine Office, 206; images of, 231; and kerygma, 45; linguistic styles of, 60; and Lord's day, 212; and witnessing, 106
Apostolic See, 186; and calendar revision, 224; and communion in both

kinds, 196; and language, 190, 200; and liturgical commissions, 193; and vernacular, 190
Aramaic, 35
Architecture. *See* Churches
Art and furnishings, 58, 127–54, 163, 219–22, 231–32; and liturgical commissions, 193; and norms for adaptation, 191
Art d'Eglise, L', 138
Ascension, Christ's, 179, 211
Asceticism, 157
Assembly of the Lord, 99
Assisi Conference, 49
Auden, W. H., 18, 61
Augustine, St., 22–23, 25, 26; on sacraments, 74
Ave (Stravinsky), 150

B-Minor Mass, 144
Baker, Father Aelred, 29–30
Baldachinos, 227
Baltimore, 22
Baptism, 78, 179, 201–2; by Christ Himself, 180; and communion under both kinds, 121, 196; and Confirmation, 105, 106, 202; Decree on Ecumenism on, 124, 125; of infants, 201–2; and Lent, 213; and participation, 117, 183; social implications of, 105; and symbols, 68–69
Baptisteries, 140, 221, 230, 236
"Basic Links Between Liturgy and Catechesis" (talk), 48
Bea, Cardinal, 49
Beauduin, Dom Lambert, 38, 44, 126
Benediction, 165, 166
Bergonzi, Bernard, 13

259

THE AUTHOR AND HIS BOOK

C. J. McNASPY, S.J., liturgist and musicologist, is Associate Editor of *America* and *Catholic Mind*. He studied at St. Louis, Montreal and Oxford Universities, and holds six academic degrees. He has lectured widely in universities and on television. A versatile writer and spokesman for the liturgical movement, Father McNaspy has contributed hundreds of articles to prominent journels here and abroad. He is author of *A Guide to Christian Europe* (Hawthorn), and co-author of several volumes on liturgy. Father McNaspy is a board member of the North American Liturgical Conference; national chaplain of the Liturgical Arts Society, and vice-president of the Catholic Art Association. In addition, he serves on several national liturgical committees.

OUR CHANGING LITURGY was composed by Harry Sweetman Typesetting Corp., Inc., New York City, and printed and bound by the Montauk Book Manufacturing Company, Inc., Harrison, N.J. The text type is Baskerville, one of the most popular book faces in modern times. The face used for the chapter heads is Lydian Cursive, designed in 1940 by Warren Chappell, a draftsman, illustrator, typographer, letterer and author. Lydian can be recognized by its short ascenders and descenders, large lower-case letters and the hooklike flourish on some of the capitals.

A HAWTHORN BOOK